REFUSE
TO BE
DENIED

REFUSE TO BE DENIED

My Grand Slam Year

SAM WARBURTON

With Steve James

**SIMON &
SCHUSTER**

London · New York · Sydney · Toronto · New Delhi

A CBS COMPANY

First published in Great Britain by Simon & Schuster UK Ltd, 2012
A CBS COMPANY

3 5 7 9 10 8 6 4 2

Simon & Schuster UK Ltd
1st Floor
222 Gray's Inn Road
London WC1X 8HB

www.simonandschuster.co.uk

Simon & Schuster Australia, Sydney
Simon & Schuster India, New Delhi

Every reasonable effort has been made to contact
copyright holders of material reproduced in this book. If any have
inadvertently been overlooked, the publishers would be glad to
hear from them and make good in future editions any errors
or omissions brought to their attention.

A CIP catalogue record for this book
is available from the British Library.

Hardback ISBN 978-1-47111-308-6

Typeset by M Rules
Printed in the UK by CP Group (UK) Ltd, Croydon, CR0 4YY

To my granddad, Keith Kennedy,
who passed away in December 2011.

Contents

1

Tipping Point

The French had a six-man line-out. I was standing in the scrum-half position, as I often do on defensive line-outs. I knew they had a move from the tail of the line-out, with their scrum-half peeling round and the blindside winger coming in at pace. And I knew I might have a split-second decision to make: to take the scrum-half or the winger.

It all depended on Dan Lydiate in the back row, and whether he was available to make a tackle. He is often used as a lifter at the line-out, but not on this occasion, as No. 8 Toby Faletau performed that task on Alun Wyn Jones, who competed with Julien Bonnaire for the ball.

Bonnaire won the ball, and I heard Dan say 'Go' as he lined up scrum-half Morgan Parra. As Dan hit Parra, the ball was popped up to winger Vincent Clerc.

In that split second Clerc was suddenly mine. You can't go into a tackle half-hearted, because that's when you'll get injured, so I used the same amount of effort as if I was tackling an 18st lock. I went in with that much force. The trouble was that Clerc is only 14st 2lbs, while I'm 16st 2lbs; I was met with very little resistance.

Clerc went flying up in the air. I panicked. What to do now? Hold on to him and the chances were that I'd drill him into the ground in a horrible spear tackle. I did not think he was that far off the ground, so instinctively I dropped him. He hit the ground and I immediately competed for the ball. I actually won it, and had it in my chest thinking: 'That's a great turnover.'

The next thing I knew all hell had broken loose and I was receiving an uppercut from one of the French second rows. Players were rushing in from everywhere; lots of the French players were in my face. Clerc was still on the floor, holding his head and making rather a meal of the incident. I looked at him and thought: 'This could look a lot uglier than it actually is.'

The referee was Alain Rolland. He blew his whistle for a penalty and stood aside from the melee. Once I'd extricated myself from the huddle of bodies, some threatening violence, others trying to prevent it, I walked over to him. He had blown his whistle immediately so I knew I was the only player he wanted to speak to. I thought it was going to be a straight yellow card. I put my hands up in apology and said to him that there was nothing malicious in what I'd done.

But he wasn't listening. He simply put his hand in his

pocket and pulled out a red card. A red card! It was the 18th minute of the biggest match of my life, a World Cup semi-final against France at Eden Park in Auckland, and I, the captain of Wales, had been sent off.

I did not protest. Indeed I thought only of one thing. I thought of the huge telling-off my mum had once given me when, after being penalised in a televised Under-20s World Cup match, I had clearly been seen swearing. I won't write what I'd said here, because my mum would only get upset again, but let's just say that it rhymes with clucking bell. I wasn't going to be caught doing that again.

And I knew there was no point arguing. In football, when yellow and red cards are given, the players argue with the referee. But it's always too late; referees are not going to put the card back in their pocket. There was nothing I could do. I just lifted my head briefly to the heavens, turned on my way and walked off.

As I passed our kicking coach Neil Jenkins, he asked me what I was doing and I said, 'I've been sent off.' He asked, 'Yellow?' And I said, 'No, red.' He went ballistic and threw his water bottle to the ground in disgust. I remember the shock on his face. He was not alone. So many people, including the TV commentators apparently, did not realise that I had been sent off.

But I had. And before I knew it I was sitting next to Bradley Davies on the bench, with a cameraman metres from me, watching my every movement, wanting me to swear or slip up with millions of people watching. Every time I looked up to see the score or how long was left in the game I seemed to see myself on the big screen: the captain of Wales sitting on the sidelines while his team tried to win a World Cup semi-final. I was going through hell, and that cameraman wasn't helping one bit.

By now there were all sorts of thoughts flying through my head: 'Have I lost the semi-final for my country? Was it my fault? Will people think it was my inexperience? Was I too pumped up? Have I let my country, my family and my team-mates down?'

I was still worrying about many of these things weeks later. Andy McCann, the sports psychologist who was at the World Cup with the Wales team, is a trusted friend, and during a quiet visit to his house in Cardiff I asked him to be brutally honest about what he thought of my mental state going into that game. He told me that I had been in the best shape possible.

During the early stages of my career and certainly during the World Cup, I went to see him every morning of a game. We would do what we call a 'mental primer' for fifteen minutes: a period mainly of visualisation, say, of the stadium we are about to play in, of specific situations that might occur in the match, and of specific personal actions, like maybe a defensive tackle or a run with the ball in attack.

That morning of 15 October 2011 had been slightly different, though. It was such a huge game, but I remember thinking: 'Why am I not nervous? I should be really.' I felt so good that I very nearly didn't go to see Andy. But as I had been doing that before every game I thought it would be presumptuous not to do so now. As usual the first thing he did was ask me how I felt. Normally I would have said that I was experiencing a mixture of nerves and excitement. On this occasion I just said: 'I feel great. I don't feel nervous at all. We're going to win.'

He was delighted. He told me that this was what he had been aiming for: the time when I was so confident in myself and in my team that I felt we could take on the world. And that was how I felt as I left his room that morning in Auckland. I could not wait to show the world how good we were.

Andy was also in the changing room before the game, and he said that I had talked calmly and that I was focused during the warm-up and anthems. Then during the short time I was on the field he said that he didn't think that I was frantic, that my head was always up and that I was making good decisions.

I thought I'd had a good start to the game. I'd felt sharp. I remember the France No. 8 Imanol Harinordoquy was about to pick up off the base of a scrum early on, and I was thinking, 'Go on, mate, do it, I can't wait for you to pick that ball up.' He tried to hand me off, I ran him about 10 metres to the side, put him down, got up, competed for the ball and it felt great. Then I had a carry of my own. I knew the boys were behind me. I was thinking: 'Stay on your feet as long as you can, they will come and pump you through these guys.' I'd just felt so good.

*

5

All of which made sitting on that bench so hard. The camera was there for the whole of the first half, but I didn't want to look like a child who'd lost his toy, so I managed to hold it together. I'd dreamed about a match like this since I was fourteen, and I was gutted. It was so frustrating because you just feel helpless. In my mind I was cheering the team on, but I wanted to be out there with them.

Then the big screen stopped showing my face and instead showed the replay of my tackle. It did look bad; it looked ugly in fact, so much more ugly than it had felt at the time.

And it became an ugly match to watch. France won 9–8 in the end through three Parra penalties, but even though we were down to fourteen men and had lost prop Adam Jones to a calf strain after just nine minutes, they played no rugby at all. We made only 56 tackles. They made 126.

The efforts of the boys were truly remarkable. We had been 6–3 down at half-time when I made my awkward way to the changing room. I didn't speak to the team because I simply wouldn't have been able to. I sat in the corner, listening. There was, of course, a general feeling that we had been hard done by. Just to lose Adam would have been enough of a blow. He is a rock for us at tight-head prop, and, with no disrespect whatsoever to Adam's replacement, Paul James, who is an excellent prop and scrummager, if there is a team against whom you want your rock at the scrummage, it is France. We'd already lost Rhys Priestland before the game to injury, then with my sending-off as well, things had really gone against us. Despite all this, forwards coach Robin McBryde spoke passionately, remotivating the team superbly.

The response was magnificent. It was heroic stuff. When we scored the only try of the game through Mike Phillips just before the hour mark, it seemed that we could pull off a victory that would have defied all the odds. You just shouldn't win a World Cup semi-final when you're down to fourteen men for so long.

But Stephen Jones narrowly missed the conversion of Mike's try that would have put us ahead, and that was it. Not another point was scored in the match. Poor Leigh Halfpenny just missed with a mammoth kick from halfway, against the wind too, which dropped under the bar. At the end we went through twenty-seven phases and still could not engineer one final scoring opportunity. It was agony all round.

What could I say afterwards? Phillsy was one of the first to put his arm around me at the end, saying: 'Don't you dare think that what happened was your fault. It's been an honour to play with you in this tournament.' That meant the world to me. I was so upset, yet at the same time I was so happy that he had said that to me.

One by one the other players did the same. What a wonderful group of blokes. They were all unbelievably good about it. I think they just knew that I wasn't that sort of player. I'd never been sent off before. I'd only ever had a yellow card playing for the Cardiff Blues.

I didn't realise until much later, but for the rest of the World Cup not one player mentioned a word to me about my red card. I don't know whether the coaches had said something to them, maybe just to make me feel better, or whether that was their natural instinct, but no one said a word.

Except defence coach Shaun Edwards, that is. A few days later he came up to me in the hotel, put his arm around me and said: 'Kid, don't worry about what happened in the semi-final. I've been red-carded before, but the difference was that I deserved mine and you didn't!' He was, of course, referring to his famous 'clothes line' tackle on Australia's Brad Clyde in the first Test for the Great Britain rugby league team at Wembley in 1994. If I'd been a bit sharper I might have pointed out that the real difference was that Great Britain won that Test 8–4, but instead we just had a good laugh about it.

There had been an incredible atmosphere at Eden Park that day, with so many Welsh fans there; some, including my parents, had made the trip just for that match. Up in the stands my mum was in tears. And I was not far off either as we walked around the ground afterwards to thank the fans.

By then I had a big black coat on, and I spent most of the walk with my hands in its pockets. It took every bit of my energy not to break down. I could see the looks of support on the fans' faces, could see that no one was holding anything against me, but I still felt as though I'd let them down. They were so good, it was almost as if we'd won. You would expect them to be just sympathetic, but you could see in their faces and their expressions how motivated they still were. Even the French fans were applauding us, as well as many of the neutral

fans too. Once I'd been red-carded, it was as if most of the stadium was behind us – one or two even left in disgust. A good
friend of mine, Brett Parry from Maerdy in Mid Glamorgan,
was one of them. He'd gone out to New Zealand with his dad
and paid an absolute fortune for his semi-final ticket, but as
soon as I was sent off, he threw his ticket in the air and walked
out of the stadium.

Afterwards our changing room was a place of devastation
and silence. I've never seen anything like it. The coaches said
a few words. Warren Gatland was full of praise. He just said
that things had been taken out of our hands, that we weren't in
control of what happened and that he couldn't fault anyone's
efforts. 'The attitude you've shown,' he said, 'is not something
you can coach. It's something that is in you.'

It was an incredibly emotional situation, so much so that
when Neil Jenkins spoke he eventually broke down in tears.
He began his speech, as he often does, about the areas of the
game that were his particular concern: place-kicking, the general kicking game, including the kick-and-chase, and the
counter-attacking of the back three and exit strategies from
our own 22. He said a few kicks had cost us; that we could
have won the game. And then it became a little too much for
him, and he had to walk off around the corner.

It was not surprising. He is so passionate about his rugby. I
always remember watching the famous *Living with the Lions*
video of the 1997 British and Irish Lions tour to South Africa
and hearing a retching sound from a certain player in the
changing room before matches. That was Jenks. And even

though he no longer plays, we still hear that sound quite often these days! While the other members of the coaching staff, Warren, Rob Howley and Robin McBryde, watch the match from the sidelines, Jenks is always on the pitch giving us water or kicking tees to the kickers. So he stays in the changing room with us to hear the final pre-match talks and shouts. He gets as fired up as the rest of us. It was obviously so hard for him to speak that night.

Even in defeat quite a few players will usually say something, highlighting good or bad things we have done in the game. That day it was only me who spoke, and I didn't say much. I knew that I didn't have to apologise. The reactions of the players and coaches had already told me that. I was trembling. I was convinced that I was going to break down in tears. But I had to speak to the players. I had to thank them for their efforts.

'I asked you before the game to be brave and give everything you could,' I said. 'And that is exactly what you did. I couldn't have asked any more of you.' I sat down. Everyone was still looking at me. I held it together.

A minute or two passed. Then the focus was no longer on me, thank goodness. I just had to be on my own. I stood up and walked around the corner into the toilet area. I went into the first cubicle, shut the door, sat down and put my head in my hands. My emotions just got the better of me. I am not embarrassed to admit that I burst into tears. I was probably in there for fifteen minutes.

It was my lowest point. Every worst thought entered my

head: 'What was everyone thinking? Was I going to be plastered all over the papers as the great villain? What were my parents thinking? What about my girlfriend, Rachel? And my twin brother Ben and older sister Holly? What about everyone who has ever helped in my rugby, from the primary school teachers who first got me into the game to the high-school teachers who helped and encouraged me so much?' To be honest, I still get upset thinking and writing about it now.

Eventually I composed myself and went back into the changing room. It was a horrible and silent place. It had been about half an hour since the final whistle and there were stunned players still sitting there in their kit.

I had a shower and, as I was changing, Simon Rimmer, our media manager, came over and asked: 'Do you want to do the press conference?' I did think about saying no. It would have been the easiest thing to do. But it was time to man up. I had to face the world and tell them that there was no malice in my tackle and that I was immensely proud of the team.

Before that I went outside into the long corridor that leads onto the pitch and sat on some steps where I phoned Rachel, my brother and parents, just to assure them that I was OK. Then I went with Warren to do the press conference.

This is the gist of what I said: 'I am gutted with the red card but there was nothing malicious. There was no malicious intent. I felt as soon as I hit him his bodyweight took control of what happened. I went to compete for the ball after, thinking it was a normal tackle and the next thing I know I was walking off into the stands. All the boys are gutted. The courage and bravery the boys showed was second to none.'

It was fairly standard stuff, so I couldn't believe it when I received so many messages the next day congratulating me on how I'd handled the situation. But how else was I going to handle it? I just thought it was the normal way to react.

On the team bus back from the stadium, first Ryan Jones, the hugely respected senior pro, and then Huw Bennett, one of the members of the tournament entertainments committee, took the microphone and stressed that we must stick together as a team. They said that as soon as we got back to the hotel, everybody must meet in the team room and have a drink together. And that's what we did, trying to have a bit of a laugh and to put some perspective on what had happened.

Not that I had an alcoholic drink, of course. We'll come to that later. And I did not stay long. The disciplinary hearing regarding my tackle was going to take place the very next day, so we had to prepare our case. For the next couple of hours I sat with Warren, Rob Howley, team manager Alan Phillips, Simon Rimmer, our head of communications John Williams, our legal representative Aaron Lloyd and a couple of representatives from the New Zealand Rugby Football Union. We went through the video of the incident and they asked me for my thoughts as we figured out what we were going to say at the hearing. I was still in my official WRU suit and I desperately wanted to go and see my parents, but we had to do it because I still wanted to play in the third-place play-off on the following Friday.

My parents were staying around the corner from the team

hotel so we eventually met in the coffee shop of our hotel. To say that they were both livid was an understatement. They had flown over specially and were meant to be my lucky charms! Mum was more angry, but I don't think she'll mind me saying that she doesn't understand rugby as well as Dad. He was gutted, but he could appreciate that, by the letter of the law, it was a red card. Mum was just furious and felt sorry for what I was going through.

It was great to see them at this hugely difficult time. It had been a long trip, a long time away from home, and to see them during the week of the game had been terrific. I remember the phone call from reception telling me they had arrived. Wow – it was like Christmas morning when you're about to go down-stairs in the knowledge that all the presents are under the tree. It was surreal seeing them on the other side of the world, with me playing in a World Cup. They had been picked up at the airport by Trudy Gatland, Warren's wife, and she looked after them royally during their stay.

I think their presence contributed to my relaxed frame of mind beforehand. All those games with my family thousands of miles away, and at last knowing that they would be only some 30 metres away in the stands was hugely reassuring.

Dad and I went up to the coffee shop counter to order some drinks. The bloke serving us was friendly and wanted to talk. 'Where are you two from?' he asked. 'Wales,' I replied.

'Did you see the game earlier?' he responded instantly. 'You'd think that the captain would know better than to dump that guy on his head, wouldn't you?'

You couldn't have made it up. My dad was kicking me under the counter. I would have liked to point out that I hadn't actually dumped Clerc on his head. In fact I would have liked to have said a few other things. But I didn't want to create an awkward situation. 'Yeah, it was shocking, wasn't it?' I replied. 'What was he thinking?'

A few minutes later my dad says that there was a commotion at the counter when a couple of the other staff were obviously pointing out to the guy who served us that the Wales captain was sitting in the corner with his parents. We didn't see that bloke for the rest of the hour or so that we were in there!

The following day I went with Warren and Aaron Lloyd to the hearing. We could only drive so far, so we parked up and had to walk through the streets of Auckland to our appointment.

As we walked, dressed smartly in our tournament-issue suits, we went past a side street where there must have been 50 to 100 supporters having a good time. There were some Welsh fans amongst them, but there were also shirts on show from many other nations. Suddenly some of them saw us and started cheering. They were all saying what a joke they thought the decision had been.

It was a truly humbling, but also strange moment for me. This was not just about me and Wales. It was at that moment that I realised the magnitude of what had happened, of how many millions must have seen the incident. How was it that a lad from Rhiwbina in Cardiff had become involved in such an episode?

I still have people coming up to me now saying that it wasn't a red-card offence. That is even though I said myself in my first round of interviews after I'd got home that I thought it was the correct decision. I was under no pressure to do that; it was just the way I felt. 'Looking back and looking at the law book, it was the right decision,' I said. 'I didn't have a leg to stand on!'

Please excuse the pun, because it was Clerc who didn't have any legs to stand on at the time, but I really didn't have a leg to stand on. I know that it was nothing personal from Rolland. He's a world-class referee, who had refereed us in three recent internationals (the summer match against the Barbarians in Cardiff, a friendly against England at Twickenham, and the World Cup match against Samoa in Hamilton). And just to prove it was nothing against me, in the week that followed my sending off, in the hotel computer room our analyst Rhys Long showed me a video of a Wasps versus Toulouse Heineken Cup match earlier that year in January when he had sent off the Toulouse centre Florian Fritz for a very similar tackle. Rolland just went straight to his pocket and pulled out the red card. That's what he does, whether it's a World Cup semi-final or a Heineken Cup match.

An International Rugby Board directive before the tournament had stated: 'Foul play – high tackles, grabbing and twisting of the head and tip tackles to be emphasised, with referees to start at red and work backwards.' My tackle was a tip tackle. And if I wasn't well versed in the laws before (and I did have a PE teacher at my school, Whitchurch High in Cardiff, called Gwyn

Morris, who was a referee and gave me a copy of the laws when I was seventeen so that I could bend them as an openside flanker!), I am now, especially with Law 10.4(j). It reads: 'Lifting a player from the ground and dropping or driving that player into the ground whilst that player's feet are still off the ground such that the player's head and/or upper body come into contact with the ground is dangerous play.'

What is so annoying is that there was no intent whatsoever. I still have some feelings of unfairness about the whole thing. Yes, in hindsight it was against the letter of the law, but I just never thought I'd be in that situation. I'll be totally honest and say that I was not sure of the law. I thought that you could pick people up and put them back down, although not on their head obviously.

In the previous match, the quarter-final against Ireland, I had made a couple of similar tackles on Stephen Ferris and Ronan O'Gara. The one on Ferris in particular lifted him way above the horizontal, but Luke Charteris came in to finish the tackle and Ferris went to the ground relatively safely. That is the way I tackle sometimes.

The hearing was the worst two hours of my rugby career. Rolland wasn't there. He just sent a statement saying: 'Tip tackle by Wales 7'. Warren told the hearing that I was one of the cleanest players he knew, even though I play in such a hostile position at openside. One of the arguments we used was that the team had probably lost because I'd been sent off, and wasn't that enough of a punishment already? Our people had, of course, stressed to me beforehand that they were not trying to make me feel bad. They were just trying to make sure I was able to play in the third-place play-off. For this was what this hearing was about. It was all or nothing for me. The length of the ban didn't really matter; if I had any sort of ban at all, it would mean that I missed that game.

I talked about the tackle, about how I felt, and explained why I wouldn't make a tip tackle deliberately. I found myself biting my lip again. I told them that this match was something I had been dreaming about since I was a young lad. That this was why I had sacrificed so much as a teenager, missing the nights out, the alcohol and all the fun. It was why I trained during every school lunchtime, and after school too; why I ran late at night and spent hours in the family home's garage with my brother Ben on the multigym that we had been given when we were fifteen. It was all geared towards playing for Wales and being the best rugby player in the world. Why would I ruin all that by deliberately dump-tackling some-body – something I had never done before in my career – in such a big match? I was so proud walking out for that match – why would I throw it all away? Hadn't I been humiliated enough by having to sit on the sidelines, a camera in my face, watching my side lose a World Cup semi-final?

It was emotional. And it was torturous. They watched the tackle from lots of different angles, showing little sympathy. To me they seemed to show it from the worst angles an awful lot. There was not one break during those two hours. It went on and on.

Eventually we were told that we could leave the room while

they decided upon their verdict. Half an hour later we were called back in and told the outcome.

The judicial officer Christopher Quinlan ruled that the offence was what they call 'mid-range', which apparently has an entry point of six weeks, but they reduced my suspension by three weeks because of my disciplinary record and remorse. It meant I would be able to play in the Heineken Cup for Cardiff Blues, but at the time all I could think of was that I couldn't play for Wales the following Friday.

I made a short statement afterwards: 'Obviously I'm very disappointed, but all my attention and focus now goes towards the players playing on Friday and supporting them the best I can.'

And that's what I did: I trained with the team all week. I think it surprised a few of the travelling press corps when I turned up to training in my full kit, but I just tried to be as normal as I could.

The match on the Friday was against Australia, as we discovered that day when they lost to New Zealand 20–6. We then lost 21–18 to Australia. It was another hugely brave effort. I think it summed up the attitude we had shown throughout the tournament that we scored a try through Leigh Halfpenny with the last play of the game, after some thirty phases. We simply never gave up.

But Australia were the better side on the night, with David Pocock having a fine game at openside, and Toby Faletau filling in at No. 7 for us and giving everything.

It was all over, and the team flew home on the Saturday morning, no more than fifteen hours after the game had ended.

I had to stay on, however. On the Sunday was the World Cup final, and then on the Monday was the IRB awards dinner at the Vector Arena in Auckland. The team management had asked for four players to volunteer to stay on for that event. There hadn't been too many hands appearing in the air for that gig, and I couldn't blame any of them really. Like everyone else I just wanted to get home.

The only reason I did stay was because my parents were there. I know I was captain, but I still think that I would have pushed hard to go home given what had happened. Toby agreed to stay as well because he was going on to Tonga (where he was born) to see family anyway. Warren, WRU president Dennis Gethin and his wife Jan, and chief executive Roger Lewis and his wife Christine made up our stay-on party.

That period until the dinner was actually a really enjoyable time. My parents came and stayed in my room at the hotel because I'd been sharing with Dan Lydiate and we'd both had double beds. So we did a lot of sightseeing together, spending a brilliant day at Waiheke Island, going up Auckland's 328-metre-high Sky Tower, and eating some lovely meals in the evening. This despite the fact that everybody now seemed to know who I was; we were even coming back in a taxi one night and drivers were beeping their horns at us and shouting out of the windows.

This was all new to me. I'm shy, but I think I deal patiently with the attention. I always make time to talk to people, and I always sign autographs and pose for photographs if I can. But sometimes there is someone who just doesn't think, and there was one such inappropriate moment when we were having a pizza one evening. I'd just taken a huge mouthful and some bloke came up and sat down alongside me, put his arm around me and asked his mate to take a photograph. I smiled and did it, but that wasn't right. There is a time and place for everything, and sometimes I just need to relax and have some privacy with my friends and family.

I went to the World Cup final with my parents, which was an awesome experience. We were in a hospitality box with all its wonderful food and drink, and Sir Richard Branson was only a few yards away, with his special All Black shirt with a number 7 and 'Sir Richie' on the back.

By backing New Zealand and their skipper Richie McCaw, Mr Branson was just about behind the right side. They won the final 8–7, but it was a far from convincing performance. Indeed, France played miles better than they had all tournament. They might even have been the better side on the day as the Kiwi nerves seemed to fray.

But New Zealand just made it, with a second-half penalty from replacement fly-half Stephen Donald, their fourth choice in that position and a man who had been fishing rather than training only a couple of weeks before.

The awards dinner was also a huge event, and it was an experience to meet up with so many players, current and former. The All Black lads had certainly celebrated their win well, rightly so, and a few of them were nursing some hefty hangovers. I met the flanker Jerome Kaino and had a really good chat with him. He'd had an excellent tournament and could easily have received the player-of-the-year award in place of Thierry Dusautoir, as he was one of those short-listed along with New Zealand's scrum-half Piri Weepu and centre Ma'a Nonu, and Australia's flanker David Pocock and scrum-half Will Genia.

Roger Lewis also introduced me to two former World Cup-winning captains in South Africa's Francois Pienaar and Australia's John Eales. Straight away Francois said, 'That red card was a shocking decision! I felt so bad for you.' He went into great detail about the mechanics of the tackle, explaining further how he considered it the wrong decision.

I already knew that he had strong feelings on the subject because I'd been told to watch his half-time television studio comments in the France semi-final. 'It was a dangerous tackle, yes. A penalty, yes. Never a red card,' he'd raged. 'Sam Warburton has been one of the cleanest players at the World Cup. He (Rolland) has killed the game. I'm livid ... It is dangerous, but this is a World Cup semi-final with all the world watching. You have all the technology at your disposal, why not go to the video referee or ask your touch judge?'

Thanks, Francois! And all the time we were speaking John Eales was agreeing too. I found it so strange. From about ten years of age I'd played *Jonah Lomu Rugby* on PlayStation, and I'd always been Francois Pienaar. Now some twelve years later, here I was talking to him and he was sticking up for me.

He was there to be inducted into the IRB Hall of Fame

along with eighteen other legends of the game, including David Kirk, Sir Brian Lochore, Nick Farr-Jones, Bob Dwyer, Kitch Christie, Rod Macqueen, Martin Johnson, Sir Clive Woodward, John Smit, Jake White, Gareth Rees, Agustín Pichot, Brian Lima and Jonah Lomu.

Eales had been inducted in 2007, but was there as chairman of the adjudicating committee for the awards. It was certainly a glittering event, made more so by the fact that it was also celebrating 125 years of the IRB. I enjoyed it in the end, if I'm honest.

But then at last it was time to go home. From Auckland to Brisbane, then to Dubai and Heathrow, and finally back to Cardiff.

I went to the airport at Auckland and the first thing I noticed was that the French team were there too. I didn't really want to talk to them. I just went to the other end of the lounge and sat on my own. Well, I didn't actually. Some lady from Wales recognised me and came and put everything right in Welsh rugby for me. She was lovely really, and I suppose it was better than talking to the French players.

I let everyone else get on the plane first, and kept my head down as I walked up the aisle to my seat. By now I was aware that there were quite a few French players around the area where my seat was. Then as I reached up to put my bag into the overhead locker I heard a few of them giggling.

I was to discover why very quickly. There was only one seat left, at the back of the plane in the middle row. And there, seated next to it with a cheesy grin on his face was none other than Vincent Clerc. What were the odds on that? Clerc and Warburton in 50D and 50E? Someone from the Emirates airline was having a right laugh.

Now everybody was laughing, including me. I sat down and shook Clerc's hand. I said bad luck to him about the final and said how well they had played. He just said: 'If you don't mind, can you give me a massage on my back please?'

I laughed again, as did all the other French boys who were eavesdropping. And that was the only mention either of us made of the tackle. We asked each other about holidays and how long we had off when we got home. We exchanged a bit more idle chatter, and then I put my headphones on and, if I'm honest, pretended to go to sleep.

I was still a bit raw and fragile about the whole thing. I did get up out of my seat a little later and talk to a couple of the French boys who were standing around the aircraft, Thierry Dusautoir in particular, who had been given that player-of-the-year award at the awards dinner. I congratulated him on that magnificent achievement.

We got to Brisbane and were waiting for our connection to Dubai (the French team would go on to Paris from there, while I would head for Heathrow) when a call came over the tannoy for me. I'd been desperately hoping for this. Earlier in the tournament I'd been introduced by Alan Phillips to Richard Vaughan, one of the top men in the Emirates airline company (currently Emirates divisional senior vice-president [commercial], so I'm told), who just happens to have been born in Tonyrefail in Mid Glamorgan. I met him again at the

IRB dinner and as we parted he said: 'I'll try to sort you out with a decent seat on the way home.'

He'd certainly done that. I'd been upgraded to first class! What a bonus. I could not believe how plush and luxurious it was. The food was top class and at last I could relax. There were still some of the French management in there, but I just wanted to be on my own now. I pulled the privacy divider across, lay back and reflected on what had happened to me over the last couple of weeks.

I recalled a conversation I had had with my mum after the semi-final. I am not superstitious, but she is. Sometimes, though, I have these weird feelings when I am convinced I am going to being proved right.

And I remember telling my mum that I was not as sad as I thought I should be after my red card. I was almost guilty about my feelings, but I think it was because I knew that I didn't deserve it. I knew that it wasn't meant to happen, and that it would even itself out eventually. I also knew that as a team we were going to achieve something great.

Or was that Grand?

2

Reluctant Captain

Let's go back to midday on Monday 9 May 2011. The domestic season had finished and I was at home in Thornhill in Cardiff, thinking only of an upcoming week's holiday in Portugal with my girlfriend, Rachel. My mobile phone rang and the name that flashed up was Warren Gatland. 'What does he want?' He might be the Wales coach, and I'd just had a decent Six Nations campaign, but it's not as if we speak every day. He came straight to the point. 'I was calling to see if you would like to be captain against the Barbarians.'

I was speechless. Then I laughed. Warren remained silent on the other end of the phone. All the while I was thinking: 'I hate captaincy.' Yes, hate is a strong word, but I still think it was the right word at that point in time. It was how I felt towards being the leader of a group of rugby players back then. And so this request from Warren, as flattering as it was, was exactly what I didn't want. I'd never for one second considered being captain of Wales.

I had been captain of the various age group sides in which I'd played for Wales – well, after the Under-16 age group, when my fellow Whitchurch High School pupil Phil Williams, now a centre for Cross Keys, had been captain. But even then I hadn't liked doing the job. In fact one day before an Under-19 international in 2007 against England at Aberavon, I phoned the coach, Justin Burnell, and told him I didn't want to be captain. I didn't like any aspect of the job, I told him, from people light-heartedly calling me 'Captain Cymru' (a comic book character) and 'Capitano', to having to make lots of decisions.

Luckily that game was called off minutes before kick-off because of the weather. But I remember talking to my parents after that and saying that I would do the captaincy through the age groups because it might help me stand out as I tried to progress through the Cardiff Blues Academy, then that would be it: no more captaincy.

And that was the way it had been ever since. But now I was being asked to captain Wales. I was standing in the front room of my house, looking into the mirror above the fireplace, while the Wales coach was waiting for an answer. I knew I had to do it. It's not something you can ever turn down. It is an immense honour. 'Yes, of course I'd love to do it,' I said, while battling a flood of very different emotions.

'Are there any media duties?' I asked.

'There is a media conference at the Millennium Stadium in half an hour,' he replied.

Flippin' heck. I rushed upstairs, grabbed a Welsh Rugby Union T-shirt from my wardrobe, slipped on some tracksuit bottoms and trainers and rushed out of the door. Luckily I had a hands-free set-up in my car so I could phone my parents, my brother and Rachel to tell them that I was going to be captain before they found out via the media. That had happened before with selection for the team, and I'd felt bad about it. So I made sure that I made quick calls to each of them. Unfortunately I could only leave a message on my parents' answerphone. I had tried.

I was rather worried. And that was before I discovered that I was to be Wales's youngest captain since Gareth Edwards did the job as a 20-year-old in 1968.

Actually, 'petrified' might be a better word. A 22-year-old with just fourteen caps suddenly elevated to captain? You'd be petrified too. 'Is this a ridiculous decision?' I asked myself. 'Am I ready? What will the other players think?'

I got to the stadium. It was no usual press conference for a relatively low-key game. All the TV and radio channels were there, along with the written press. The match was not until 4 June, and it was only the squad being announced, not a specific starting line-up, but there was a big story. And thankfully it was not just the word 'captain' after the name S. Warburton.

Gavin Henson was back. Even though he'd not appeared in an international for more than two years and had only started three club matches since April 2009 (and had just fallen out with his club Toulon), he was being given another opportunity for Wales. All the media wanted to talk about Gavin.

They even asked me about him, though I hadn't picked the team. And I had to say: 'It is hard for me to talk about him, because I haven't met him before. Warren says he is a professional guy so I am sure that is the case.'

There were of course questions about the captaincy. 'It was a massive surprise when Warren rang me up and told me,' I said. 'I can't wait to lead the side out at the Millennium Stadium and it is going to be amazing. It is an achievement I thought would never happen. So to happen at the age of twenty-two and after just fourteen caps was a surprise, but I am looking forward to it. Everyone would love to be captain of Wales but it was something I thought would never happen so soon. I captained the Under-19s and -20s at World Cups so I have a little bit of captaincy experience. There are also plenty of leaders in the squad who can help me out.' I thought it best not to mention that the thought of captaincy filled me with dread!

I was, however, interested to hear what Warren said about me, and the reasons he offered for giving me the captaincy. 'Sam is an excellent professional and was one of the Six Nations stand-out players . . . If you were looking at a Lions side now his name would come up as a seven.'

Wow. That was high praise. 'There are other leaders in the squad like Alun Wyn Jones, Ryan Jones and Stephen Jones that will support Sam in his role,' he continued. 'Matthew

Rees [who had been captain during the Six Nations campaign that preceded this match] has done magnificently as captain, but he needs a break. It is a good chance to give Sam some responsibility in terms of leadership. He is well respected by the players in the squad and that is the first example you are looking for. He also keeps himself out of trouble, which is a bonus!'

It was pleasing to hear such words, but it didn't change the fact that I didn't really want to do the job. I was still seriously nervous. There were already loads of congratulatory messages on my phone, which made me feel very proud, but I was way out of my comfort zone here. I went home and spoke to Rachel and my parents, told them all about these concerns and fears. This was not going to be easy.

I can only apologise to Rachel for the way I behaved on the holiday that followed the captaincy announcement. It was only our second holiday away together, but I just couldn't relax. Every day I woke up thinking about being captain of Wales, about what I was going to say to the players. Did I have to be like Winston Churchill before the game? What about the after-match formalities and the inevitable captain's speech? That was putting me off more than anything else, although I didn't admit it to anyone – not even Andy McCann. I thought it was better left unsaid, and I'd see what happened on the day, although when we'd returned from holiday I threw up in the bathroom because I felt so nervous.

Once on holiday I got up in the middle of the night and started making notes about things that I thought might be useful to say to the players. 'What are you doing, Sam?' asked a bleary-eyed Rachel. 'Please just switch off!' I couldn't. I went to the gym every day, sometimes twice a day, and always ate healthily.

If there was any comfort it was that I thought this was just a developmental decision. I was never going to be captain in the long run; Matthew Rees was. I could do it once and then never again. Maybe Warren was doing this to bring me out of my shell.

Whenever I am feeling nervous, under pressure or lacking in confidence, there is always one person I know I can talk to. Andy McCann, our sports psychologist, has been a great influence and a huge help to me in my international career. Warren first used him in 2009 with the Wales team. 'The use of a psychologist is a personal thing,' Warren said. 'Andy will not be involved in any team stuff, but he is there if players want to talk on an individual basis.'

And while Andy is superb at talking to large audiences – he is a very successful and widely used conference key-note speaker – he is also brilliant on that one-to-one basis. I can talk to him in the same way I talk to my brother Ben.

I first met Andy properly at the after-match dinner of the Wales versus Scotland match in Cardiff in 2010. We got talking, and I soon realised that he was one of the most interesting people I'd ever met. I told him that I had some confidence issues regarding certain aspects of my game, especially my carrying of the ball in attack at that time. We did some work on it and I found out he could do a lot more for me, with techniques like relaxation and visualisation, and he soon became a vital part of my match preparation. He can make my confidence sky-high when I'm playing for Wales, and it definitely has a knock-on effect on the pitch. I also see him for relaxation through the week, so I can get a good night's recovery.

I rely heavily on Andy, and I know there will be people who do not think that is good, who do not believe in the benefits of sports psychology. But it works for me. We train our bodies relentlessly, but the mind is just as powerful. So my view is that we need to train that too. I feel very comfortable in Andy's company and he has a calming influence upon me. That's the sort of character he is.

Andy had been a PE teacher and competed, coached and refereed to international level in martial arts, but in 2004 at the age of thirty-seven he suffered a stroke while taking a class. 'Within seconds I had become a heaving, helpless weak wreck that was unable to move. I had been transformed from a fit, athletic physical education teacher and martial art instructor instantly – or to use a more appropriate term, at a stroke,' he wrote in his award-winning book *Stroke Survivor*.

He has done more than survive, of course. He has made a remarkable recovery – and I can vouch for that. When I had an injured calf during the autumn internationals of 2010 I did a grappling/boxing/wrestling fitness session with him for about 45–50 minutes and he completely dominated me! At one stage he had me pinned down, unable to move in the form of a human pretzel. My T-shirt was drenched at the end of that session.

31

But none of this is surprising, given his strong and positive personality. In 2005 he resigned from his teaching post and went into business. He now runs his own corporate training and consultancy company.

Andy lives in Cardiff, so not long after I'd returned from my holiday I went to see him. I told him exactly how I felt about the captaincy, about my fears and insecurities about being handed the role at such a young age.

As he always does, he made me feel better. And he had an idea. He suggested that we come up with a leadership compass. It is a technique used in business to give leaders a better understanding of themselves and what they expect from those they are leading. It is your very own model for leadership. Each direction of the compass has a quality from which you can draw strength and support. These are the four qualities I decided upon:

1. Professional attitude
2. Positive attitude
3. Develop personal relationships with the players
4. Most importantly my own performance, and leading by example

I saved this compass on my iPhone under 'Notes' so that I could read it regularly. It became my model for captaincy, which I could go back to time and time again in those early stages. By the time of the Six Nations Championship in 2012 I didn't use it at all, but back then, in those nervous, uncertain times, it was an enormous help.

I also had a lot of help from Derwyn Jones, the 6ft 10in former Wales second row who is now my agent and manager. He came to my house for a coffee and I confided in him that I didn't want to do the job. He too calmed me down. His experience of having played at the top level was invaluable, as were his times as team manager of Cardiff RFC and the Ospreys. He knew what most of the players I was about to captain were like, so he could offer informed advice on how best to handle them and what to expect from them.

Soon, though, it was time to go into camp for the match. I'd been to our team base in the Vale Hotel in Hensol, the Vale of Glamorgan, many times before, but this was a very different experience as I went there as captain. We met up, had breakfast and went through all the medical screening that we usually have when gathering after a break.

Warren then called a team meeting. He spoke first, in particular to congratulate those who would be making their debuts against the Barbarians in this match to celebrate the 130th anniversary of the WRU: Scott Andrews, Ryan Bevington, Lloyd Burns, Toby Faletau and Scott Williams. Then he asked me if I wanted to say anything.

I hadn't planned anything, but I could hardly say no, even though I'd rarely spoken in team meetings before. I think a lot, but say little. Off the top of my head (or maybe that midnight notes session in Portugal had been useful!), I said, with passion increasing all the time as I spoke: 'I think in the past couple of years good performances that have not resulted in wins have been accepted a little too easily. Losing cannot be an option in any game. We've got to perceive ourselves as favourites. The Baa-Baas will be on the piss all week, do a couple of half-hour training sessions and probably turn up full of alcohol. It would be unacceptable and embarrassing to lose to them. After this we don't play until we face England in a World Cup warm-up in two months' time, so it's just one game that we have to give everything to. Let's be professional and get on a winning run.'

I was glad to get that first speech off my chest, and I was really pleased when Andy came up to me afterwards and complimented me on how well I'd spoken. Yet although every player came up to me at some stage during training that week and congratulated me on being made captain, I still felt embarrassed. I was only twenty-two and there were lots of senior players around; I could imagine some of them saying behind closed doors, 'It's a joke Warby is captain.'

I had some good advice from Adam Beard, our Australian head of strength and conditioning. He stressed that I should not get too caught up in the whole captaincy thing. He said that I still had to make sure that I looked after myself, that I had to focus as hard as ever on my own conditioning and nutrition and not worry too much about the team.

And on Facebook I had an important message. It was from Tom Shanklin, the Cardiff Blues, Wales and British Lions centre who had been forced to retire from rugby only the previous month with a knee injury. It said: 'Congratulations on the captaincy. It was always a tag I put next to your name when you were coming through the Blues.'

I'd had no idea that anybody had been thinking that way

about me at the Blues. But it made me feel a whole lot better that someone of Tom's standing in the game had said that. If I had his approval, then maybe I had the approval of the senior players in the Wales squad.

What I definitely didn't have, though, was a room-mate. Traditionally the captain has his own room, and so for that match against the Barbarians I awoke at the Vale with no one to talk to. It was horrible. I vowed then that it would never happen again, and ever since that match I have always shared a room.

I was always going to be nervous on the morning of that Barbarians match, but being alone made it much, much worse.

At that time I was doing a 'mental primer' with Andy on the morning of each match. That morning of Saturday 4 June 2011 I went to Andy's room and knocked on the door. He could tell immediately that I wasn't quite right. Usually there was that mixture of excitement and nerves, which is healthy. On this occasion there were just nerves. It was all there for Andy to see. 'I'm crapping myself,' I admitted. 'It's the most nervous I've ever been.'

When I'd first started working with Andy he'd suggested that it would be a good idea to settle upon a personal identity statement, which we could use at times like this, when I needed reassurance and focus. The statement we had agreed upon was: 'I am the world's best seven.'

I hope this doesn't come across as arrogant. It is meant to reflect my ambition and desire. When I was at school Gwyn

Morris always told me that I should aim that little bit higher, even if it appeared unrealistic at the time, because then you might surprise yourself with what you might achieve. In every match I play I have to consider myself better than my opposite number. Playing for Wales against some of the best openside flankers in the world, that means I have to consider myself the best in the world, otherwise I would be beaten before I start. I have always wanted to be the best seven in the world. That has always been my aim.

Andy has a recording of the noise and atmosphere at the Millennium Stadium in Cardiff that he plays for me during our sessions. I close my eyes and in my mind I am in the Millennium Stadium. I am actually out there on the pitch. I remember Andy saying some time later that he saw me take one big intake of breath, as if I was actually out on the pitch. Because I was so nervous that day he had to help me a lot with my breathing techniques, while repeating my personal identity statement.

He really had to work hard on that particular morning. I was in a right mess. I felt all eyes were on me. And it was not just the captaincy – it was also the fact that I was in direct opposition to Martyn Williams, who had been picked at openside for the Barbarians. Of course, I was the man in possession of the Wales No. 7 jersey, but this was a great opportunity for him to stake his claim for the World Cup. He was one of my heroes as I was growing up, and, of course, one of Wales's greatest ever players. I still watch tapes of his play now because I think the attacking side of the openside has been forgotten about. Everyone talks about the defensive dominance at the breakdown and being able to compete and win the ball, but I think Martyn's support play and handling skills are better than any other seven in the world. And that's the side of my game that I've been trying to work on. He'd been the first player to speak to me when I turned up for my first day's training at Cardiff Blues and we even ended up doing a weights session together that day.

The fact that I was playing against Martyn and was captain for the first time was a dangerous cocktail. I just couldn't control my nerves.

Thankfully Andy worked his magic. Within fifteen minutes he had calmed me down. More than that, he had made me so confident that I wanted the game to begin there and then. It was a shame there were another three or four hours until kick-off.

We lost to the Barbarians 31–28. After that big talk of mine that it was unacceptable to lose to a group of players more interested in socialising than training. And I blame myself. It was my fault, and I'm still disappointed about it now.

We lost from the final play of the match. We had been 28–19 up with just six minutes to go, after we had scored tries through George North, Morgan Stoddart, Mike Phillips and Aled Brew, all converted by Stephen Jones.

Samoan second row Iesofa Tekori, Leinster's Fijian full back Isa Nacewa and Italy's Sergio Parisse had scored tries for the Barbarians, with Clermont Auvergne's Australian-born Brock James converting two of them. And although the France centre

Mathieu Bastareaud scored a try for the Barbarians, we were still leading 28–24 with a couple of minutes to play.

It is obvious in those circumstances that you stick the ball up your jumper and keep it, Barbarians game or not. We weren't trying to play like the Barbarians; we were trying to win. We were trying to make Stephen Jones's 100th cap a memorable one. Despite what I said about the Baa Baas enjoying themselves, they had a very good side, captained by Parisse and including the former All Blacks Doug Howlett and Carl Hayman, South Africa's Joe van Niekerk and Australia's George Smith, who replaced Martyn in the second half.

So we had a line-out in their half. And we had a training-ground drill that we practise with defence coach Shaun Edwards all the time. It is called the 'one-minute drill'. Nothing fancy or clever about it: all you have to do is keep the ball for one minute. Here all we had to do was two of those in succession. In other words, keep the ball for two minutes and then boot the ball off the park!

The team was gathered around, and that was the message that was relayed. Ryan Jones was playing in the second row, and he ensured it was made forcibly too. The call was a banker call to the front of the line-out, and we began rumbling forwards. We kept it easily for about five phases, and then, as I was getting up from a ruck, I saw something I simply could not believe. The ball was being passed from scrum-half to fly-half. Why? We didn't want to play. We didn't need to play.

I screamed 'No!' as loudly as I could. But it was too late. The ball had gone. And, surprise, surprise, we lost it. We knocked on. And Willie Mason, the Australian rugby league legend who was about to join Toulon and who had come on for the last fifteen minutes in only his second match of rugby union, took advantage. He'd already produced a moment of magic for Bastareaud's try and now he began a move that, thanks to a remarkable off-load, saw Nacewa score his second try. James converted and the Barbarians had won.

In terms of personal performance I thought I'd done reasonably well against Martyn in our personal battle, but I was absolutely devastated. I had lost my first game as captain. I had let Stephen down on his big day. That was far more important than anything to do with me. We should also not forget that we observed a minute's silence before the match for the four people killed in the Pembroke oil refinery tragedy that week.

I thought I was going to be slated for my inexperience. I could already hear Ceri Sweeney piping up at training at the Blues. He sometimes used to call Martyn 'Captain Crap' because Martyn's win ratio in charge of Wales was not good. He captained them eight times and lost six. Now Ceri was going to be saying the same about me. It was only one game, but often the team jokers need little invitation.

It was a mistake that still haunts me today, and one I will never make again. I'd obviously not made completely sure that everyone in the team knew what was going to happen.

Within an hour of the match finishing a 45-man training squad for the summer had been announced to the press.

Gavin Henson was in it. He'd had a decent, if not outstanding, game, but he had set up George's early try. There was no mention of a captain.

After I'd done the post-match press conference I went to the family room in the Millennium Stadium. I'm ashamed to say that I could barely speak to my family. It was 70 per cent down to losing and taking the blame, but also 30 per cent because I was dreading the after-match speech so much. I even remember thinking about the speech once when I was still on the pitch towards the end of the game. That shouldn't be happening!

Paul Tito, the popular ginger-haired Kiwi second row and my Blues colleague, played for the Barbarians that day – as did scrum-half Lloyd Williams, who came on in the second half for the Frenchman Sebastien Tillous-Borde – and he had been ribbing me all week about my speech and how he couldn't wait to hear it. I know he thought that I was going to be an absolute shambles.

In the end, I don't think I was too bad. I reckon I surprised a few people that night, and maybe even myself too. I knew I could do it; it was just that I hated the thought of it. I did all the usual thank yous, then elaborated on the game by saying congratulations to Stephen as well as all the new caps that day. It all went down well apparently, but it did not matter anyway. I was not going to be doing that job again.

Or so I thought.

3

Evil Saunas

We had been given plenty of warning. We had begun summer training about ten days after the Barbarians match, and for just under two weeks we had trained hard at home in Cardiff. It was made very clear to us that we had to be in the best shapes of our lives by the time the World Cup arrived in September. Warren Gatland felt that we weren't able to play the game he wanted us to, so we needed to be stronger and fitter.

But, as hard as we trained, all we kept hearing from Adam Beard and our other conditioners was: 'Poland will be harder.'

It was pretty daunting. Two camps were planned at the Olympic Training Centre in Spala, and only Andy Powell had been there before with Wasps. Warren had obviously been there with Wasps too, but there was little point asking him about the finer details of the trips. He was never going to tell us, and if he did, he'd probably exaggerate. So we were busy quizzing Andy as to what it was going to be like.

The truth is that nothing could have prepared us for these trips. 'Savage' was the word I used at the time to describe the ferocity of the training, and nothing has happened since to soften those feelings.

As for the cryotherapy chambers which allowed us to do so much more training than we would normally be able to do, well, the chapter title says it all. My first impression was that they were 'evil saunas', and I stand by that description.

The centre in Spala has gained a very good reputation over the last few years. As well as the cryotherapy chambers it has an athletics track, a grass rugby pitch, an indoor swimming pool, weights facilities, tennis, basketball and volleyball courts, and all the medical facilities for physiotherapy and other treatments.

But it is not the Vale Hotel, which is what we were used to. In fairness we get pretty pampered there, with lovely rooms and excellent food. Spala was not going to be like that. Both the accommodation and the food were going to be very basic. The management were on the lookout for players who might crack and break. They wanted to get rid of any negative people. This was going to be a real test for all of us.

It was a very quiet coach that took the by-then 42-man squad to the first camp. Since the announcement of the summer training squad the Scarlets hooker Ken Owens had been added as cover for the injured Richard Hibbard, and Lloyd Williams had been brought in for Mike Phillips, who had been suspended after a well-publicised late-night incident in Cardiff city centre.

But from that original squad of forty-seven, five could not make the first trip to Spala. Stephen Jones was missing because of the impending birth of his first child, Hibbard was still injured (shoulder), as was Morgan Stoddart (thigh), although he eventually came out to replace Jason Tovey who had a back injury. Sale would not release Dwayne Peel, and Gareth Delve was still out in Australia with the Melbourne Rebels.

I shared with Gavin Henson in the hotel near Heathrow the night before our very early flight to Warsaw. As I said before the Barbarians match, I did not really know him, so this was an experience I enjoyed, especially as I could ask him about *The Bachelor*, the TV show which he had been filming. All the boys were keen to hear about that!

But before we knew it we were up at 4am and off to Warsaw. I knew it was going to be a tough trip, but I got off to the worst possible start. Spala is situated in central Poland and is about 60 miles from Warsaw, but that coach trip from the airport seemed more like 600 miles to me.

Yes, it was through some scenic if sparse countryside – a flatter version of the Brecon Beacons is how I described it at the time – but I had a problem. I needed the toilet desperately. Of course, there was no such facility on the coach, and I just did not want to ask for the coach to be stopped. It had already been a really long day and I knew that the players just wanted to get to Spala, so I hung on for nearly two hours. It was horrific.

When we eventually arrived at our destination I sprinted off the coach in search of a toilet. The only problem was that I had left my iPhone and iPad on the coach, which promptly drove off. I got them back about four days later – what a start!

In fact that experience worried me so much that when a trip to the World War II concentration camp at Auschwitz was planned later during the stay, I did not go for fear of getting caught short again on a coach without a toilet! Instead I stayed behind with Lloyd Burns and Toby Faletau and went on a shooting trip in some nearby woods.

There was some time off amid the race to become the fittest Wales team of all time. There was a pizza place near the training centre that took a real hammering on our days off. We were burning so many calories during the training that it was hard to eat enough, and just before a day off you could hear the boys saying, 'Tomorrow is pizza day ...' Mind you, it might have been because the other food we were getting was so different from what we were used to that the pizzas seemed so good. Maybe one day I'll go back there on holiday and find out. Or maybe not ...

A typical training day, mostly meticulously planned by the excellent Adam Beard, panned out as follows: the wake-up call was at 6am; breakfast was at 7am; then at 8am was our first training session. That was always the hardest one of the day. We were split into three groups: the back three and centres were together, as were the half backs and the back row, and then there were the front five.

Waiting to do your session was torturous. You'd be in the

team room, sometimes overlooking the session, and there would be rumours flying around as to what was going to be involved. Then you'd see the state of some of the players returning from their session. They would be covered in sweat and sand; some might even have sick on their shirts – it was that ferocious. I remember turning up to a session one day and seeing Josh Turnbull, who is one of the fittest boys in the squad, throwing up on the side of the track. And we were all thinking: 'Oh my God, we've got this session to come!' Just as there had been on the bus on the way, there was always a fearful silence as we walked to those sessions.

They would start relatively comfortably. There would be twenty minutes of work with the sprint coach Frans Bosch, a Dutch bio-mechanist who had previously done work with Northampton and England, especially with the winger Chris Ashton. Frans does not just do simple sprint training. His big things are motor control and the economy of running. He and the other conditioning coaches cannot believe that I can run as fast as I can, with the running style I've developed over the years. So they have been trying to teach me how to run, giving me special exercises to strengthen specific muscles around the hip, core and glutes to help me run more quickly.

Then after Frans had done his work, there would be a fitness circuit for some thirty to forty-five minutes. This was where it could start getting messy. One circuit was what I can only describe as 'mental'. It is too complicated and arduous to describe in detail, but it included such exercises as cleans in a sand pit holding really heavy bags, pushing even heavier sleds, wrestling shirt-on-shirt, tug of war, tyre flips, sprinting, and 'down and ups'. It was ridiculously hard. By the end of it I was feeling dizzy, and as I finished my last exercise, pushing a sled on the grass pitch, I collapsed onto my chest on the grass.

'Thank God it's over,' I thought. Or not, according to Dan Baugh, the former Cardiff and Canada flanker who is now one of our conditioners, having just joined full time from the Cardiff Blues before this trip. 'One more circuit,' he said. At that moment I was actually annoyed. I train as hard and as religiously as anyone, but I remember thinking, 'This is just too hard. We're being pushed too far here.' But one more circuit we did.

And there was more. Yes, more. Next we played 'King of the Ring' – one-on-one wrestling in the volleyball sand pit – just 'to finish you off,' as Dan Baugh said.

To make it even more competitive, Warren Gatland and Rob Howley were standing there watching. They were clearly trying to get into our heads because they were talking just loud enough for us to hear. On one occasion I was wrestling against Jonathan Thomas and I could clearly hear Warren saying to Rob: 'I reckon Jon Thomas will win.' It was clever stuff. There was no way I wanted to lose in front of the coaches.

There is so much respect for all the coaches from the players. They all help us in their different ways. Warren is obviously the head man and so commands huge respect. He has had a massive impact on my career, and I can't thank him enough for taking the risk to make me captain at the age of twenty-two, even if I didn't necessarily think that at the time. He has given me so much confidence in my ability and, without wishing to put down the coaches I worked with before, he has taught me more in the last couple of years than I learned in the whole of my rugby career before that. I think all the boys agree that he is a superb coach and person. We were certainly a happy group of players when it was announced that he had re-signed until the end of the 2015 World Cup.

Rob is the attack coach and he works a lot with me and the back row on little things like our running lines off the fly-half. He and Neil Jenkins also do a lot of handling work with the forwards. Rob will hit tennis balls at us with a racquet to improve our hand–eye co-ordination, and Jenks will work hard at receiving kick-offs with us. My handling skills have definitely improved a lot because of the work I have done with Rob and Jenks.

As for Shaun Edwards, he is the tough northern guy who has taught me so much about defensive play. When I first played for Wales, I will admit that I was incredibly naïve about what real defence meant. Shaun has worked hard with me to explain defensive structures, always taking me aside after games and showing me what I could have done better, pointing out where I could have missed out on hitting a ruck and maybe folded into the defensive line, or vice-versa.

Shaun has his own way of coaching tackling, and especially encourages us to keep our hands up and tight to our body before throwing a shoulder at the last second at the man to be tackled. I remember once doing a session with him and Dan Lydiate, and practising just that. Shaun was emphasising that we almost needed to do an uppercut as we performed the tackle. So as he turned round to talk to Dan, I was behind him practising my uppercuts. The only problem was that I didn't realise that the session was being filmed. Some time later a film was made by the analysts of funny things that had happened, and, no surprise, that clip was on there. It looked like I was being really keen, out on the field, all on my own, doing uppercuts to please Shaun. Embarrassing!

In our group out in Poland for the 'King of the Ring', the two winners were Dan Lydiate and Ryan Jones. They were both in there for ages, and when they fought each other it was an extremely competitive wrestle. Dan is a complete strength freak, but Ryan has long levers and is deceptively strong in the close-contact stuff. By the time they had finished their three minutes in the 'ring' they both looked absolutely spent, both covered in sweat and sand and with their shirts ripped.

There were players shouting, screaming and swearing. It was full-on stuff. There were lots of other athletes staying and training at the centre, and some of them must have been walking past and wondering what on earth was going on. We actually got word from some of them later that they had never seen a group of athletes train as hard as we did during our time there.

Justin Tipuric, the Ospreys flanker who was to make his international debut later that summer against Argentina in Cardiff, was a dark horse in this 'King of the Ring'. He may not be the biggest but he is very clever in contact, and when Alun Wyn Jones ran at him he soon had him pinned to the floor. I was very wary of Justin. He is an openside flanker too, of course. The competitive spirit is always strongest when you're up against someone after your place!

At the end of that first session, which sometimes included some anaerobic rugby-based games devised by Dan Baugh, we would also do twenty minutes of skills work. It might be something like tennis-ball work or passing drills, but at this stage there was no set-piece rugby work. That would come later, in the second Poland trip, which had a little more emphasis on rugby than this first one which was all about fitness and conditioning.

It didn't help that it was so hot, as it appears that Poland, contrary to a lot of people's perceptions, does have continental summers. We were to go there again early in 2012 and experienced very different weather, but during the summer camps it was so hot that, after these morning sessions, Dan Baugh would often cool us down afterwards, as well as clean off all the sweat and sand, with a hosepipe on the grass pitch.

Then it was back to the room for a shower and a protein shake, and maybe some snacks. We were only fed officially three times a day in the training centre, but we really needed to eat six times a day, so there were special sports meals, a bit like Pot Noodles I suppose, as well as protein shakes, bars and lots of fruit always available in the team room.

At 11am it was time for our first cryotherapy of the day, followed by maybe twenty minutes of recovery on the exercise bike, and then at noon it was lunchtime. You have to shower and dry thoroughly before you can go in the cryothcrapy chambers, otherwise the moisture will freeze over, or, as Toby discovered, if you leave your hair wet and you have an Afro, it will set hard!

At 1pm came our second session of the day: a technical weights session under Adam Beard's supervision, with the emphasis on power, with lots of squats, cleans, deadlifts, bench presses and chins. Adam has to take a lot of credit for the way he organised the training. He was superb in his thinking and the choice and use of exercises. As he often says: 'Other teams will be fit, but we are rugby fit.'

That was followed by another protein shake and more snacks, and at 4pm a second bout of cryotherapy. At 5pm we had dinner, and then finally at 7.30pm was the so-called 'Hypertrophy Club', another hour-long gym session but with much heavier weights. This was very much Dan Baugh's 'baby', as they say. This was his chance to shine, this immensely strong and powerful guy, more so than any of the players actually, even though he'd retired from playing with the Cardiff Blues to become an assistant conditioning coach in 2005. The last I heard he was bench pressing 200kg for four repetitions. That is awesome.

The players really respect him because he is sympathetic towards those who have chronic injuries, particularly with shoulders and knees because he had those sorts of injuries himself. And the physios love having him on board because he is the crazy guy who can do all the contact work for them. So, if a player is coming back from a shoulder problem, for example, instead of him being thrown straight back into contact work with the rest of the squad he can do some controlled contact work with Dan. And Dan doesn't mind if you smash him. He is just a block. I remember running full pelt at him once – no shoulder pads or tackle shields, just bone-on-bone – and he was the one picking me up off the floor rather than vice versa. He is invaluable to the squad.

Dan would write about five circuits up on the board, and you'd have to pick one and off you'd go with a partner. Tops were allowed off in this session – Andy Powell needed no second invitation! – and there was music blaring from the speakers. It was really good fun, the best session of the day, and the boys really looked forward to it.

Sleep wasn't actually on the schedule for the day, but whenever there was the odd hour between sessions there was only one thing I was doing, and I'm pretty confident that most of the other boys were doing the same! You had to sleep, otherwise you'd be seriously flagging. And you had to be in bed by 9pm as well. Not because that was a curfew time; simply because you had to get nine hours' sleep to be in any shape to cope the next day.

Normally if you tried to fit all the training we were doing into one day, you'd be in trouble. You'd be no good to anybody the next morning. But here we were going into breakfast, saying how good we felt, that we were ready and able to do it all again. And that can only have been down to one thing: the cryotherapy. We had used ice treatments in recovery before, plunging into a huge horse box filled with freezing water at the Vale, but this was taking things to a whole new level.

The chambers are basically freezers for humans. We had to cover up our extremities and wear special gloves, shorts and socks to guard against frost-bite. There were also masks to put on to enable you to breathe because the air in there is too cold to take into your lungs. And the chamber is full of dry ice, as you might expect, and this is what makes it reminiscent of a sauna, albeit a particularly painful and evil one.

There is a big industrial door into a pre-chamber that is like a fridge, so that cold air is not lost from the main chamber. The main chamber is very small, with only two spotlights inside and a tiny window to peer out of. If somebody puts their hand over the tiny lights – which, of course, a couple of the team pranksters did – it is suddenly pitch-black and absolutely horrible.

The chambers can go down to minus 160°C. On the first day the temperature was brought down to minus 120°C and we had to stay in there for two and a half minutes. That was gradually increased during the trip. So by day four the temperature was down to minus 140°C and we were staying in there for four minutes. Some Olympic track and field athletes who use them regularly stay in for five minutes, but any longer than that is considered dangerous.

I'll freely admit that my first experience was an extremely nervy one. It is seriously claustrophobic in there and it didn't help that a senior member of the squad banged on the door and window and pleaded to be let out. Until now I've never revealed the identity of that member, but considering he has now retired from the game, this seems an appropriate time to do so.

It was Martyn Williams. He did stay in on all the other occasions, but just that once he panicked. And quite naturally he got a lot of stick from the boys for that. Not that his actions in any way diminish my total admiration for him. He is a Wales legend and everybody recognises that. I thought the world of him before I met him on that first day of Blues training, when Chris Tombs, one of the conditioners, said, 'Sam, your training partner is Martyn Williams,' and I think twice as much of him now.

Chris has looked after my training programmes since I was about fifteen and in the Blues system, and he has also always looked after Martyn's. So he knows both of our bodies inside out. We have slightly different programmes to suit our individual needs, but to be able to train with Martyn was just amazing.

I remember the first time I played alongside Martyn for the Blues against Munster at the Arms Park in May at the end of the 2009 season. It was a Magners League match that we eventually won 20–12, and I was wearing the No. 6 shirt and Martyn his usual No. 7. It was only my third match for the Blues, having made my debut away at Edinburgh at the beginning of the previous month as No. 8.

Fly-half Nicky Robinson had just kicked a penalty for us in that match against Munster and I was jogging back to our own half. Alongside me was Martyn, chatting about what we should do from the kick-off and what Munster might try to do. I had a bit of a Eureka moment. It suddenly dawned on me that I was playing alongside Martyn Williams. It had always been my ambition to do that on the Arms Park, and here I was living the dream.

I also desperately wanted to play alongside Martyn for Wales. That wish also came true later in 2009 when I came on against Australia at the Millennium Stadium to replace Dan Lydiate to play at blindside flanker, with Martyn at openside. Sometimes we would swap over, if one of us had just done a particularly hard bit of work on the openside, so that the other could take over briefly.

I am very proud to have played alongside Martyn for the Cardiff Blues and Wales. I'm also pretty proud that I didn't do the same as Martyn and scream to be let out of the cryotherapy chambers on that first attempt. I was so close to doing that.

In the end we tended to go into the chambers together to help each other through. We would share the window, cupping our hands against it because by then the man in charge outside knew us and he would put the clock timing our session next to the window so that we could see how long was left.

Each session was generally done with four or five players in the chamber at one time. So Justin Tipuric and Toby Faletau would also come in with us, because they are calm and reserved characters. What you didn't want was to be in a group with the likes of Bradley Davies, Josh Turnbull, Dan Lydiate and Lou Reed, because you knew they would be mucking around, screaming deliberately, blowing on your chest (which gave you this weird feeling of ice hitting you even though it should be relatively warm air coming out of your body) and pulling your shorts down.

Obviously, as soon as you go in the cold hits you and you have to keep moving just to be able to stand it. But then your skin temperature begins to drop and you can see the ice form on the hairs of the boys' chests and you start to feel pain searing round your body.

There were various tactics to try and make the time go more quickly. At first some would put their hands on each other's shoulders and dance around, even singing at times. There were a few renditions of Tom Jones's 'Delilah', and I have a distinct memory of Gavin Henson singing the Backstreet Boys' 'I Want It That Way' pretty well too.

At other times the boys would play word association games. Someone would say football, then I'd say Tottenham Hotspur, and the bloke next to me might say Ledley King.

Of course, I would say Tottenham Hotspur because I am an avid Spurs fan, and not just because I was in the same class at Whitchurch High as the current Spurs star Gareth Bale. In fact there were plenty of future sportspeople at the school. The rugby league international Elliott Kear was also in my class; then there was Geraint Thomas, the Olympic cycling gold medallist (although I didn't know him as he was a couple of years older than me), as well as Sarah Thomas, my girlfriend Rachel's sister, who plays badminton for Wales and went to the Commonwealth Games in Delhi in 2011. Tom Maynard, the future Glamorgan and Surrey cricketer, was in the sixth form with me, playing in our rugby team that won the Welsh Schools cup. While I was writing this book I received the tragic news that Tom had died aged just twenty-three. I still can't believe it. He was such a popular and sociable guy.

My dad is from London, and from the age of six I was a Spurs fan. In the family photo album there is a picture of me and Ben both wearing full Spurs kits. I had 'Sam No. 9' on the back, he had 'Ben No. 10'. As my dad always says, 'Once Tottenham, always Tottenham,' and if I had to play in any stadium but the Millennium in Cardiff, it would be White Hart Lane. At the family home in Rhiwbina, Cardiff, we have two Shetland sheepdogs called Ted and Gus, named after Teddy Sheringham and Gus Poyet.

Anyway, back to the word association game: if you couldn't think of a word you had to crouch down lower because it was even colder down there!

By days four and five, though, we had worked out that you could take your iPhones into the chambers without them getting damaged, so the theory was to find a song that would last the time you were supposed to be inside for (four minutes by then). That certainly helped with the pain we were going through. I'd be lying if I didn't say it was a pretty savage experience, but the other side of the coin is that it definitely worked and allowed us to train in a way that would have been impossible under normal conditions. The cryotherapy dampens the nervous system, flushing the toxins away from the muscles so that you come out feeling fresh.

We were basically packing what would normally be deemed

two intense days' consecutive training into one fourteen-hour period. Apparently we had our highest ever ratio of players fit despite all the training we were doing – there were no muscle pulls or anything like that, and that can only have been down to the cryotherapy as well as the great work of the medical staff, the physios Mark Davies and Prav Mathema (not to forget Craig Ransom who stayed at home to look after those not on the trip), and the two massage therapists Angela Rickard and Lukasz Kuzmicki (who is Polish but has worked in Wales for us too). Lukasz acted like a second team manager behind Alan Phillips. 'Thumper', as Alan is universally known, is really good at his job, but his skills don't quite extend to a knowledge of the Polish language, so Lukasz did a lot of sorting and chivvying of the locals.

The relationship between the players and the backroom staff was really superb, as it was between the players and coaches. So much so that at the end of the World Cup the players decided to chip in to buy gifts for John Ashby, the conditioner, and Angela. They both worked so hard – especially in the evenings when Angela would often miss meals because she was tending to aching bodies – that we all felt they both really deserved it.

The video analysts, Rhys Long, Rhodri Brown (both of whom went on the British and Irish Lions tour of South Africa in 2009, as did Prav Mathema as physio) and Andrew Hughes, are all brilliant at their jobs, working long hours too, and fitting in really well with the players. Rhys has been head of performance analysis for the Welsh Rugby Union since 2007, having been with Wasps before that. Apparently he was a decent player – a No. 8 for Welsh Schools and Bridgend – before having to retire through injury and concentrating on performance analysis.

Rhodri has worked with Wales since 2004, and Andrew joined in 2006. Prav is a much more recent addition to our team, having joined in 2011 after being at Wasps and before that at Queens Park Rangers FC. As well as revealing a highly professional work ethic, Prav has also shown an interesting liking for surprising people – by leaping out on them, that is. Be careful when you go round a corner if Prav is in the vicinity – that's the motto. He also loves table tennis, as does Neil Jenkins.

Prav is the relative newcomer, while Mark Davies is the stalwart. 'Carcass', as he is known, has been with the Wales team since 1999. He played for Wales, gaining three caps as a flanker between 1981 and 1985, and is hugely respected, even if the boys can't help taking the mick whenever he takes the microphone on the team bus to advise of impending physio appointments. His voice is rather nasal, shall we say, and is quite easily imitated. He gives as good as he gets, though, as does Professor John Williams, the team doctor, who in the summer of 2012 left his post to become the WRU's Sports Medicine Consultant. 'Prof' surprises a few of the players when he gives them some stick back. They don't really expect it from a doctor, but it helps him fit in really well.

Then there is John Rowlands, 'JR' to all. He's the baggage man and has been for donkeys' years. Bradley Davies always teases him that he is pretending to work, but he runs around like mad helping the players out with everything. He helps the coaches out too, mainly by providing Kit Kats and sweets for them, all neatly lined up on the table alongside our protein drinks. Like me he's from Rhiwbina, and he reckons I'm the second hardest guy from Rhiwbina – after him, of course!

This Wales camp truly was a happy one, so it should come as no surprise that, even amid this hardship in Poland, there was fun to be had. We had to generate it ourselves, because the Spala training centre is in the middle of nowhere and there was absolutely nothing to do. So every four days Gethin Jenkins was in charge of a pub quiz. He'd be busy on the Internet finding questions and splitting everyone up into teams who would then select silly names for themselves. He's got a massive music library so there were naturally plenty of music questions. Everyone would put in £10 and the winning team would share the pot. There was plenty of humour and banter, with someone like Mike Phillips causing much amusement with his ability to take the mick out of himself. There was a round of questions on brands, and it was announced that one of the answers was 'Stella Artois'. 'I think I had that one covered,' shouted Phillsy, in reference to his recent escapade in Queen Street, Cardiff, as everyone burst out laughing.

There was only one rule for these quizzes: be in Adam Jones's team. He was unbelievably good. I don't think any team with him in it lost. He was the same when he was on *Question of Sport.* They said he was one of the best they'd ever had on that show, and I can well believe them.

When we were in Hamilton during the World Cup later

that year, we had another of these quizzes courtesy of Gethin, and I happened to be in the winning team along with Jamie 'Doc' Roberts. We won $300 or so, but decided to go to the casino next door and put it all on red. We were both really nervous, as we're usually pretty careful with our money. We would never normally do that sort of thing and haven't done so since then. We were well out of our comfort zone, but we went for it and it came in for us – happy days!

Throughout the Poland trip there was a lot of banter flying about because the World Cup squad had not yet been picked, and indeed some players were going to be left at home when we returned to Poland for the second camp. So anybody appearing to presume that they were going to be on that second camp or in the World Cup squad was cut down to size immediately.

There would be silly questions like 'Will you share a room with me in New Zealand please?', and if you said yes, the reply would be an astonished, 'So you're in the World Cup squad already, are you?' It was an ongoing joke of the sort I'm sure all professional sportspeople, gathered together in close environments for long periods of time, indulge in from time to time.

One evening I was nearly caught off guard. I was walking back from my 'Hypertrophy Club' session when I saw Jamie standing outside the team room. He looked fairly serious and asked if I had a minute. He said that the backs, who had been waiting to do their hypertrophy session, were just sorting out some dinner arrangements. It was obvious that James Hook and Shane Williams were his main accomplices. Often during home campaigns we will go out for a team meal at somewhere like the Caesar's Arms in Creigiau just outside Cardiff, and prior to that a choice of about four main meals will be listed on the board for you to put your name under your choice. 'Doc' (yes, he is training to be a doctor) said that there was a big meal planned at a posh steakhouse for the next time we were in Poland and that they were getting things organised early. He was very plausible, and at first I believed him. I went into the room where all the backs were lounging around and taking no notice of me whatsoever, studied the meal options on the board, took the pen and was just about to write my name down when I twigged. I turned around and every person was looking at me, just about to erupt into laughter and abuse. They hadn't got me. Nearly, but not quite.

So I was in the joke now. Who could we get? It just so happened that Scott Andrews, the Cardiff Blues prop, was the next man to pass the room. He was duly called in, believed the story, scanned the options and made his choice. One of the options was a mixed grill, which was clearly not quite as healthy as some of the others. He took the pen and put 'Bubba', his nickname, under the mixed grill option. Not only had he fallen for the joke, he'd chosen the least healthy option – you should have heard the abuse!

I actually feel a little bad about this because Scott was left behind for the second camp. We had just five days at home before we set off back again to Poland, and this time Stephen Jones was with us, but along with Scott, players like Andrew Bishop, Ken Owens, Andy Powell, Lou Reed, Richie Rees,

Jonathan Thomas and John Yapp were left at home.

That a couple of them, Powell and Owens, ended up going to the World Cup shows how quickly things can change, something Warren admitted at the time: 'The door is still very much open for those players who are not making this trip,' he told the press. 'This camp will have a strong focus on rugby while retaining the skills and conditioning elements of our first visit to Spala. It will give us further opportunity to see more of some players, in particular in an intense rugby environment, with the likes of Ryan Bevington, Lloyd Burns, Justin Tipuric and Scott Williams all gaining an extra opportunity to show us their worth. The nature of the training regime next week meant we were always going to take a smaller group of players, because of the strong rugby element involved. The players on the camp have an opportunity to work hard and impress, but it will not be a case of "out of sight out of mind" for those players who remain at home.'

It has been publicised that during the summer training we had something called a 'dry board' in the team room. That was Dan Baugh's idea, because they had had something similar when he played for Canada. Basically it is an honesty call about whether you have been drinking any alcohol. Every player put in £20 at the start of the summer and those still left on the dry board at the end of the summer training could share the winnings of over £800, with over forty players involved in total. For me it was easy. I hardly drink at all; I simply don't like the taste of the stuff. I think I had one glass of wine with Rachel on holiday in Portugal in May before the summer training began – and then only because the bottle of wine came free with the meal! – and the next time I had a drink was a couple of cranberry vodkas after the third-place play-off against Australia in New Zealand on 21 October.

I remember saying to Leigh Halfpenny, who also drinks very little, that we didn't even have to try to win that. It was the best £20 bet we'd ever placed.

If you had a drink you had to come into the team room and move your name from the 'dry board' to the 'wet board'. Poor George North doesn't drink much, but he went to a friend's 21st birthday party and had one beer. He was honest enough to admit it and rule himself out of contention for the money. Others had a glass of wine over a meal with their wives or partners and they had to own up too.

There were still ten of us left at the end, although there was some scepticism amongst members of the squad that Gethin Jenkins's name was still on that 'dry board'. Not that I am casting aspersions, of course!

Not towards Gethin, anyway, but as for my mate, Dan Lydiate, well, I have to tell you that he is one of the tightest men in the world. He was one of the winners too, not having touched a drop of alcohol during the summer, but whereas all the other winners were willing to put their money back into the kitty, Dan was having none of it. He wanted his money . . .

That's my way of getting my own back after Dan playfully said at the WRPA (Welsh Rugby Players Association) dinner after winning the players' Player-of-the-Year award: 'I'm just glad that I've beaten Sam Warburton for once!'

We also had another board up. This one had three categories: the Liabilities, the In Betweeners and the Webb Ellises. The idea was that if we could get everybody into the latter category we would have a good chance of winning the World Cup: the Webb Ellis Cup.

I was put in the Liabilities section straight away because I turned up for the summer training slightly underweight. They'd wanted me to come back at 16st 4lbs, but I'd arrived weighing only 15st 9lbs. At the end of the 2011 domestic season I had been up to 16st 7lbs and had not been happy with it. I had injured my knee early in the last match of the Six Nations Championship out in Paris, so during my rehabilitation period I had been advised to bulk up and really try to put some weight on.

I have never eaten so much. I was having huge pizzas as afternoon snacks, and cooking big chicken breasts at the same time to spread on top of those pizzas, just to add extra protein. I was eating huge meals late at night, and so by the time I started playing again I was heavier than I had ever been before.

I made my comeback for the Blues against the Newport Gwent Dragons at Rodney Parade where we disappointingly lost 28–15, and then we played against the Scarlets at Parc y Scarlets, where I was wearing No. 6 again and Martyn No. 7. We lost 38–23, and I just wasn't fit enough. I felt like a slug. I remember running out for the second half, and Josh Turnbull, who wasn't involved in the match but was sitting on the bench, was laughing at me because I was in such a state.

He could see that I was dying; that my fitness wasn't anywhere its normal level. I just pulled a funny face at him and jogged off.

I decided then that I needed to lose half a stone. Some players can carry that extra weight, but I don't think I can. I just wasn't as dynamic or as fit as I wanted to be. I think the Wales management realise now that I can't carry that extra weight, but at the start of that summer they were expecting very high standards, and that is fair enough. I probably had lost a bit too much weight when I turned up at 15st 9lbs.

It was not long before I was back to where I and the conditioning staff wanted me, at about 16st 2lbs, where I feel I have enough muscle bulk without being too unfit. And so I was soon in the Webb Ellis section where everyone wanted to be. I think I'm right in saying that by the end of the summer training, everyone was in that section. When we had our fitness results just before the first summer warm-up match against England at Twickenham, there were twenty-one personal bests, with a number of players smashing their old records. It was amazing to watch at times, especially some of the achievements of players like George North, Leigh Halfpenny and Lloyd Williams.

But along the way there was obviously some pain. We do something called the WAT (Wales Anaerobic Test). It's the most hated test amongst the squad, devised specially by Adam Beard to replicate rugby's demands. We start on the ground and then get to our feet, complete an agility circuit, for instance a 10-metre figure-of-eight around some cones, and then do a

20-metre sprint. And we keep going. It is a horrible exercise that makes you want to be sick.

Just like some of the training exercises in Poland, there are some remarkable sights at the end of WAT sessions. The back three are considered the fittest in a rugby team these days and so are expected to get the best scores on tests like these, so it's little surprise that it is a battle between George and Leigh as to who is the best. George was the champion during that summer training, with a time of just under two minutes, but Leigh, being the incredible competitor that he is, pushed him all the way. I remember doing one of these tests with Leigh in Cardiff and it was unbelievable how hard he pushed himself. Fully five minutes after he had finished the test he was still grunting and groaning, with his legs up against a wall and the physios rubbing his legs to try to get rid of the lactic acid. The good thing was that everyone had shaved approximately ten seconds off their best times by the end of the summer.

You could be placed in the Liabilities section for the smallest misdemeanour. It could be something minor like forgetting to weigh in in the morning, or just wearing the wrong kit. And while we were in Poland if you were in the Liabilities section you had to do a punishment. The more players in that the section the longer the punishment had to be, with five minutes added to the exercise for each player in the section. It was some punishment, because it was a session with Dan Baugh in his favourite area: the sandpit. And Dan loves giving these beastings. Apparently you'd be wrestling, doing bear crawls and generally doing horrendous fitness work on your knees in the sandpit. On one occasion Alun Wyn Jones and Ryan Jones had to do it, and they wouldn't let anyone watch because it was so horrible. Fortunately I managed to stay squeaky clean on that trip and did not have to do a punishment. Only about eight or nine players did.

When Adam Beard was accidentally late for a meeting one day, we said to him, 'We've been doing all these punishments, so it's only fair that you do!' And he had to do it for an hour. We were killing ourselves laughing. Fair play to him, he did well though. It was a gutsy effort.

As it had been from the whole squad. We had trained harder than ever before. Hard enough for a little treat on our last full day in Poland. There had been some talk amongst the players that it might be an idea if we were allowed just one beer in the bar at the end of that day as a reward for all our hard work. But the coaches, and Dan Baugh in particular, were adamant that there was to be no alcohol. That had been the stated aim since the start of the first camp.

So we finished our last session, a very tough rugby session, and we were all being hosed down by Dan when Alan Phillips was spotted walking across the field with a couple of cardboard boxes and a cooler bag. He was quickly surrounded and he opened up his boxes of goodies. There were Magnum ice creams, in both white and dark chocolate, as well as cans of Coca Cola. Heaven! We sat on the grass devouring our rewards. What a wonderful feeling.

But it was typical of those summer training trips that we

weren't finished yet. And this time it was our own fault. We were leaving the training centre in Spala before 9am the following morning, and at a team meeting that evening the question was posed as to whether anyone would like to do a 5.30am training session. Everybody said they wanted to do it. Adam is always keen for us to do these early morning sessions because he thinks it gives us a mental edge over other teams.

We were up at 5am to do a forty-minute session of rugby-related games. I think the coaches were really happy, not just at the fact that we had volunteered to do the session, but also at the quality of the session. There were very few dropped balls, and the standard of the sevens matches and other games was excellent.

We were clearly ready to play some proper rugby.

4

Decision Time

The team to play England at Twickenham on 6 August 2011 in the first of the back-to-back World Cup warm-ups was announced to us by Warren Gatland. Almost casually after my name he slipped in the word 'captain'.

I was captain again. Hooker Matthew Rees was still struggling with his injured neck and had been given an injection to try to rectify the problem. Warren must have assumed that, as I'd been captain against the Barbarians, it would not be too big a deal to do it again. He certainly didn't tell me beforehand.

Injuries meant that we were without Gethin Jenkins (calf) and Adam Jones (toe) at prop, Leigh Halfpenny was still out with an ankle problem, and James Hook was struggling with his shoulder. Otherwise Warren picked what he considered at the time to be somewhere near his full-strength side. There was little mention about me being captain in the press, mainly because Stephen Jones was about to become Wales's most capped player with 101 caps. Of course, that never happened because he unfortunately pulled a calf muscle during the warm-up before the match and Rhys Priestland was moved from full back to fly-half to begin what was an incredible journey for him, as he became a key part of our World Cup campaign at fly-half.

The big bonus for me was that I was sharing a room. I'd told Warren after the Barbarians match that I was never going it alone again, and so now in London I was paired with Dan Lydiate. He's one of my best mates and always good fun; such a positive bloke who is always high-fiving and hugging team-mates. It was just the sort of company I wanted and needed.

So I was much calmer on the morning of the game. I even went for a green tea and a bottle of water with Lloyd Burns and Toby Faletau, sitting in the sun at a coffee shop near our hotel. I bumped into Rob Howley, who told me not to worry too much about the captaincy; to be quite selfish and make sure that I did my own things well first.

But I was still worried, especially about what I would say to the players before the game. I even wrote down a few things on the hotel's notepaper. The trouble is that when you are standing in front of twenty-one pumped-up players two minutes before going out in a Test match, that all goes out of the window. You have to speak off the cuff, and for my first few Tests in charge I was not very good at doing that. I stuttered a little and never said what I really wanted to say. And I always felt I was patronising the senior players when I made those pre-match speeches.

As I mentioned before, this was not something I could admit even to Andy McCann. I was embarrassed. It was the only thing I kept from him, but when I eventually confessed to him he helped me enormously. I even went to watch him speak in public to see how he did it.

Alun Wyn Jones led us out at Twickenham for his 50th cap, and Morgan Stoddart filled in late at full back for Rhys who had moved to fly-half. And for nearly fifty minutes Morgan had an excellent match. But then calamity struck as he suffered a horrific broken leg in an innocuous-looking tackle from opposite number Delon Armitage. I was on the opposite side of the field when it happened, after we had spilled ball in England's 22 and they had counter-attacked. Morgan had then intercepted a back-handed pass from Matt Banahan intended for Armitage before he was tackled.

Apparently the television producers considered it too shocking to show replays of the incident, bringing back memories of a similar injury suffered by the Wales footballer Aaron Ramsey while playing for Arsenal against Stoke in February 2010. Fair play to the England scrum-half Danny Care, who instantly indicated to referee Steve Walsh that Morgan was badly hurt and for him to stop play. That was great sportsmanship.

We lost the match 23–19, but we finished it so strongly – undoubtedly because of the work we'd done in Poland – that it only just felt like a loss. We felt really good; so good that if the match had lasted another five minutes we would have been confident of victory. There were times towards the end of the game when we'd been through a number of phases and we'd look over at the English team (in black shirts that day) and they were blowing hard.

Don't get me wrong, they are one of the toughest sides in the world to play against, and I'm not saying they weren't fit. But it was just that we felt that we could go up another notch. Dan Baugh and Adam Beard would be coming on to the field and emphasising what we'd been through in Poland. They were saying that the way we felt was not through any accident; it was because of the way we had slogged it out in training.

Just after half-time, Manu Tuilagi, on his debut, had gone over for a try, after an inside pass from man-of-the-match Jonny Wilkinson who scored thirteen points including two drop goals. That put England 18–7 ahead. On the hour mark they were 23–12 ahead.

Many teams would have buckled. We didn't. We just kept coming. George North had scored a first-half try, put in at the corner by Morgan Stoddart and doing well to hold off Manu Tuilagi's tackle. Now Shane Williams scored after good work from Bradley Davies and a long pass from Mike Phillips. Jamie Roberts nearly scored when Rhys Priestland dinked a kick through, but the ball dribbled into touch, and then I nearly scored in the corner after a front peel from the line-out.

They don't often work, those front peels. When the coaches said in training that we were going to do it, I remember thinking, 'I'm going to get "smoked" by their hooker here.' They are a bit like that move you sometimes see when a player charges through the middle of the line-out – he often gets smashed!

So when Ryan Jones called this one, I steeled myself. I went round the front and suddenly a huge gap opened up. I went for it. But Tom Wood, on for England captain Lewis Moody, just tackled me in the corner. It was referred to the television match official, but it was never a try.

A few minutes later I nearly scored again. I had prop Ryan Bevington, on for Paul James, to thank for that. He received a pass from scrum-half Tavis Knoyle, on for Mike Phillips, and carried hard using a much-used play, whereby I was his shadow runner. The hope is that the defence jams in tight on the ball-carrier and he can release the player behind him. On this occasion it worked perfectly as three defenders converged on Ryan and his pass to me was perfectly timed. I saw James Haskell in front of me and stepped to my left and the line was in sight. Unfortunately, the England full back Delon Armitage was coming across to cover and made an excellent tackle. Lloyd Burns picked up and went close himself before the ball was recycled and passed right where we had a huge overlap. Ryan Jones took Rhys Priestland's pass and fed George, and our 19-year-old winger had his second try, putting the ball down one-handed and throwing it jubilantly into the crowd.

We outscored England by three tries to two, and they were

nervous at the end, make no mistake. There were still four minutes remaining when Rhys Priestland converted George's second try. We could have sneaked home in that time.

I was happy with my own performance, especially in that last quarter, but I'd lost two from two as captain now. Was I going to be one of those terrible captains with a shocking record? Again I was asking: 'Am I the right man for the job?'

There were already rumours that Matthew Rees wouldn't be fit for the home game against England the following week at the Millennium Stadium. I could be captain for the World Cup. Oh my God . . .

We made an important collective decision that night at Twickenham. The team had obviously had a lot of bad press over the previous year regarding drinking, so this was a good forerunner for the World Cup. We decided it was best that no one had anything to drink. With only a short turnaround, we needed to get our recovery in. The best thing was to return to the hotel and have some good food, some protein shakes and get back to it on Monday.

And that's exactly what we did on the Monday, in preparation for that return game. This was now a huge game. We simply had to win. Warren spelt that out very clearly, both to the players and to the press.

'We need the win this weekend – it's as simple as that,' he said. 'We've told the players that, for us to be regarded as contenders at the Rugby World Cup, we need to beat England at home this weekend, to send out that message to everyone that we are contenders.

Decision Time

'We have the toughest pool at the tournament [along with South Africa, Samoa, Fiji and Namibia] and in less than a month's time we will be facing South Africa in our opening match. It is vitally important that we go into that match with the sound of Welsh fans ringing in our ears, fans who have cheered us on to victories in the final two matches of our warm-up campaign against England and against Argentina next week.

'We have retained the majority of the side who travelled to London last week and told them that we want more of the same. There are one or two players we have brought in to have a look at but the reason we have deliberately not made whole-sale changes is that we need to win this game and we believe these are the players who can do that.'

There were four changes from the team beaten at Twickenham. James Hook replaced Morgan Stoddart at full back, with Morgan undergoing an operation on his broken left leg in London's Charing Cross hospital and not returning to Wales until the Tuesday after the game. Sadly his World Cup dreams were over. It was a sharp reminder to us all how cruel the game can be.

Warren had not been particularly happy with the way we had scrummaged at Twickenham, but even though Adam Jones was declared fit, it was decided to play Craig Mitchell again, and there was a great moment in the first half when we won a penalty, kicked by Rhys Priestland, after a particularly powerful and destructive scrummage. Lloyd Burns was given his first Test start at hooker, and Luke Charteris took over from Bradley Davies in the second row. Gavin Henson was also given a starting place, replacing Jon Davies in the centre.

And still there was that extra word, usually an abbreviation, in the bracket alongside Cardiff Blues next to my name: 'Capt'. Ceri Sweeney would definitely be keen to use that other word beginning with a 'C' and containing a 'P' if we lost again.

We didn't. We beat England 19–9: a remarkable win. At half-time the score was 6–6. But the other statistics in that period were that England had had 65 per cent of the possession and 75 per cent of the territory.

The bad news for Gavin Henson was that, after a good start with some solid tackles and an important tap tackle on Shontayne Hape after England had been putting us under huge pressure with a series of five-metre scrummages, he had been taken off after just under half an hour with a suspected broken arm. It turned out that he had dislocated his right wrist and required an operation. He too was out of the World Cup.

Our defence was unbelievable. Shaun Edwards had steeled us for a tough afternoon of work beforehand, telling us that if we could concede fewer than fifteen points we would win. He knows his Test rugby inside out and is almost always spot on with such assessments, and he certainly was here.

He was also right in saying that we were going to have to do some serious defending. People said afterwards that England were sloppy and lacking a cutting edge, but I don't think that paid full credit to how well we defended. It began as early as the thirteenth minute when everyone thought Matt Banahan (who had come into their side late on as a replacement for the injured Chris Ashton) was going to score, but Shane Williams, with the help of James Hook, somehow managed to keep the big Bath winger out; the tone had been set for some heroic work.

Just after half-time, Toby Flood kicked a penalty after Jamie Roberts had been sin-binned. He had tackled Mike Tindall who had caught the kick-off, steaming up to claim it between me and Toby Faletau, but Jamie had come in from the side at the ruck that had formed quickly. But despite Mike Phillips also being given a yellow card after seventy minutes for a similar offence of killing the ball, England never scored another point in the game.

Rhys Priestland had to depart injured at half-time, so that meant a reshuffle with Hooky moving to fly-half, Shane Williams to full back, and winger Aled Brew coming on. Hooky proved the match winner, scoring thirteen points including a penalty from halfway in the last minute that sealed the match, after Mark Cueto had been penalised for holding on. Hooky was the first player I hugged when the whistle went and we could celebrate a landmark win. We'd beaten the Six Nations champions, the best team in the Northern Hemisphere at the time.

Hooky had scored our only try just before the hour, wriggling between the tackles of Dan Cole and James Haskell after a good carry from Huw Bennett (on for Lloyd Burns). He converted that and then in the 67th minute kicked another penalty that looked to have sealed things at 16–9. But Phillsy was sin-binned and we had to defend for our lives as much as we had in the first half.

When I went to the World Cup, Andy McCann made me a motivational video, and it should come as little surprise that most of the defensive clips were from this game. I think I made eighteen tackles in the game, with Toby Faletau making a similar amount.

I remember one particular tackle from Dan Lydiate. It was England's last attack of the match, one of those 50/50 calls, and given that we'd already had two yellow cards (the referee was Rolland!), this could easily have been a third. Dan made a brilliant tackle and then performed what we call an 'offside jackal'. He got up on the wrong side, which, as the tackler, is legal as long as no ruck has been formed. But the ruck formed very quickly and could easily have been perceived as hands in the ruck. As it was, it won us the game.

I got the man-of-the-match award, which surprised me, but was certainly the best moment of my career at that point. I'd never beaten England before at age-group level, and had lost to them in that year's Six Nations in Cardiff, as well as at Twickenham the week before. It was a huge thing for me, as evidenced by the sixty-odd text messages of congratulation on my phone afterwards. And it was a huge thing for my family too. My dad is English, but my brother told me afterwards that Dad was in tears at the end, so I sent him a text: 'You big girl'.

There was one warm-up Test left that summer, against Argentina the following week in Cardiff. I was not involved in that. It was felt appropriate that I had a rest, and Martyn Williams took over as openside flanker and captain. He wasn't actually named as captain at first, Ryan Jones was, but he had to pull out with a calf injury, allowing Martyn to take over. It was to be Martyn's 99th cap and he was not to get his 100th until he played against the Barbarians in June 2012, after he'd retired from regional rugby. I was so glad he got that 100th cap; he certainly deserved it, and I'm sure it would have haunted him for the rest of his life if he hadn't made it to 100. I was there watching at the Cardiff City Stadium when he made his final appearance for the Cardiff Blues against Edinburgh at the end of April. It was disappointing, to be honest, because there weren't many more than 3,000 people there. A player like Martyn deserved a better send-off than that.

Also in the side to play Argentina in that last match before the World Cup were Lee Byrne, Leigh Halfpenny and Adam Jones, all returning from long-term injuries. In all there were nine changes from the side that beat England in Cardiff. Jonathan Davies returned in the centre to replace the injured Gavin Henson, and scrum-half Tavis Knoyle was given his first start of the summer warm-up matches, with Lloyd Williams on the bench, from where he would win his first cap. James Hook continued at fly-half after moving there to replace the injured Rhys Priestland against England. Warren was giving players sufficient opportunity ahead of the scheduled World Cup squad announcement on the Monday after the Argentina game. Nobody was certain how he would split the thirty-man squad between backs and forwards.

There were lots of options. 'Criteria for selection has been about putting together a side to win the game, but also about giving some players the opportunity to impress and, therefore, bid for selection for the World Cup,' he said. 'In some areas we are also looking at combinations with that opening game against South Africa on 11 September always kept in mind. Beating the Pumas on Saturday would also mean we retain that all-important winning momentum going into the World Cup. But there are still many places up for grabs on that plane to New Zealand and the players all know they need to perform against the Pumas in order to further their own as well as the national cause.'

We won the game 28–13, with tries from Andy Powell, who had a good game just before the World Cup selection, Alun Wyn Jones and George North, with James Hook kicking thirteen points. We were not at our best in the first half, but two tries just before half-time gave us a 14–3 lead which Argentina never looked like taking.

There was, though, more important and much sadder news that week. On the Monday it was announced that Matthew Rees was out of the World Cup. His neck problem was just not getting any better, so it was decided that the only solution was surgery. He was in a lot of pain with it, and was struggling to sleep at night.

I was hugely disappointed for 'Smiler', as we call him. To miss a World Cup must be awful, especially when you were going to be captain. And I'll admit it: I so wanted him to be fit and to be able to go to the World Cup – it would have solved a million worries for me.

Decision Time

Alarm bells were ringing loudly now. I could be Wales's youngest ever World Cup captain. But I didn't want to do it. I didn't want to captain Wales at the World Cup.

There, I've said it. I know there will be people shaking their heads in disbelief, screaming that they would give their right arms to do so, but that is the way I felt. I didn't want that extra pressure; I just wanted to concentrate on my own game.

I called Andy McCann. 'We've got to talk,' I said. So we met in the café at the Vale Hotel. We talked for what must have been an hour and a half. 'I absolutely hate the captaincy,' I said. Yes, that strong word hate again, but this was an emotional and difficult time for me. 'You don't understand,' I said. 'I just can't do it.'

Andy did understand, of course. As I expected, he was very good about it. He didn't tell me to do it; he didn't tell me not to do it. He said that I had to be true to myself and do what made me happy. I told him everything I didn't like about the job. I went on and on, detailing why I did not think I was a good leader. And then I told him the thing that worried me most: I couldn't tell Warren. I couldn't tell the coach that I did not want to captain my country.

So Andy said he would speak to Warren for me, which made me feel better. And later that night he texted me to say that he had done so.

The next day I had finished my gym session and was walking through the Barn at the Vale Resort (or the WRU National Centre of Excellence as it is now quite rightly called, as it is a superb facility) when I saw Warren. He asked if he could have a word. He said that Andy had spoken to him and that he hadn't realised that was the way I felt.

I told him that I was flattered that he had asked me: 'It's the biggest honour of my career.' He said, 'You said that after the Barbarians game, but did you really mean it?' I replied that yes, of course I did, but that I just wasn't enjoying doing it. I asked why he didn't want various other players to be captain. He simply said that he wanted me to do it.

I thought immediately of a chat I had had that summer with a member of the Special Forces. Let's just call him Sven. The secret meeting had been arranged by Andy McCann through his many connections. Andy thought it would be good for me to talk to Sven, as he had also been made a leader at a young age. He loves his rugby too. He'd talked about the concept of 'Confident Competence', whereby it is important to remember that if somebody has appointed you as a leader they clearly have the confidence you can do it. He took confidence from the man who appointed him and he urged me to do the same with Warren. Sven's decisions were about life and death; mine just concerned a game of rugby. It's a cliché but it did put things into perspective.

Not that I was necessarily seeing that now as I spoke to Warren. He said that they would do everything they could to accommodate me as captain. They would ensure that I didn't have a single room, of course. They would be careful of the extra pressures they placed on me (there had been a couple of occasions when I had not been happy about having to rush to afternoon training sessions – usually the most important ones – after doing media duties). They would speak to the senior players and make sure they helped me in the way I wanted. They would do whatever I needed, he said. Then he asked me to go away and think about it. And just as we finished, he said: 'You never know, if you don't do the captaincy, your sponsors might take that nice white convertible off you . . .' He smirked and walked away. He's clever like that.

I went home and spoke to my parents and Rachel. I told them that I wasn't going to do it. I didn't want to be captain at the World Cup. Writing that now, I can see why they were so gutted.

During that week there was an interesting team meeting in which we did a debrief of the England game in Cardiff. Shaun Edwards showed us a clip of our heroic defence, of us winning a turnover and a penalty. Everyone was going mad with delight. And he said: 'The captain looks pretty happy!' I was punching the air, tapping players and pulling them off the floor. I was certainly pumped up.

After the meeting Warren pulled me to one side. He showed me that clip again. He said that I was demonstrating outstanding leadership qualities in doing what I did there. That surprised me. He showed me another clip where I was talking to Rhys Priestland about a move. He also showed a few more clips of me doing things on the field that I do without thinking and have certainly never considered to be special leadership qualities.

The point he was making was that to be a leader you don't necessarily have to be pulling the guys into a huddle all the time and pointing the finger. He thought – and he was right – that I had the idea that a captain has to be very vocal. I am not vocal; before I was made captain I would sit in the changing room, read the programme and not open my mouth once.

Ryan Jones is a vocal captain, as is Matthew Rees, who will get up in team meetings and really lay the law down. I am not comfortable being like that. But I just thought there was one model for a captain and that was it. Mind you, I've known some captains who will talk at every opportunity in a meeting and give you clichés all week, but as a player I wouldn't remember what somebody said to me on a Monday morning after a session.

I think Warren might have spoken to some of the senior players that week. I think he thought I was missing the approval of some of them, because I had an answerphone message from Matthew Rees. He said we needed to talk. 'Either come up to my house in Tonyrefail or I'll come down to the Vale,' he said. We agreed to meet for a coffee in the Vale Hotel. He was to the point. He said I had to do it. And he said that I was definitely capable of doing it. That reassured me. He then went on to talk about how important he considered the little things off the pitch – like organising various sub-committees amongst the players to deal with things like fines, food and laundry to keep them all happy and involved.

That was a hugely important chat. All the while Andy McCann was talking to me, as well as Derwyn Jones. I'm not sure how he did it, but subconsciously Andy persuaded me that I should do the job. When I'd been talking to Warren I'd asked him if Andy was going to be at the World Cup. When he'd said yes, that was a huge boost to me and one of the biggest factors in my decision to accept the captaincy.

Andy really does mean that much to me. And I'm not the only one. Most of the younger guys in the squad have worked extensively with him too. 'Being the youngest in the squad and not having as much experience as others, I've relied a lot on Andy to calm me down and help me chill out,' George North said at the end of 2011. 'He's a great guy and has done a lot for me. He's given me the confidence to back myself and not go into my shell. I've met him for coffee since we've been back from the World Cup and we keep in touch. He works with a lot of the boys and what he does is different for each player. When I've been injured he's good at helping me build my confidence back up. Every morning before a game I ring him too – it's good just to hear a friendly voice. He'll just give me little things to remember on the pitch and key points to focus on throughout the game. I've done a lot of work with him and I thank him a lot.'

And Leigh Halfpenny too: 'I have worked closely with Andy, and there are different approaches,' he has said. 'There may be a switch-off session early in the week which can be helpful, and then when the game beckons I go through my roles and get them clear in my head. If I am nervous, it relaxes me. It is about being composed, and then we know we have to focus for the week after.'

I knew I had to do it now. I told Rachel and texted my

parents. They were all ecstatic. They had so wanted me to do it, and were glad that I'd now made that decision.

On Sunday 21 August 2011, I was just about to go to bed when I noticed a missed call on my mobile phone. It was from Warren. It seemed late to be making a call, but he and the rest of the management were obviously still deliberating over the World Cup party that was to be announced the next day.

'We have never been afraid to be brutal in the past and there are a few youngsters who I believe really put their hands up in the first two games,' Warren had said after the Argentina game. 'But it's not about being brutal with big names, it's about picking the best squad and that's hopefully what we'll do. There will be a lot of people who will disagree with us, but I don't think people should expect too many surprises. We've only got fourteen fit backs so if we do a 16–14 split between backs and forwards people are going to know who those backs are. If we do 17–13 then there are some who are going to miss out. The hard decision is the back row. We scrummaged well against Argentina but I didn't think we were as mobile as we were in the first two games.'

What he did not say was that he did not know who was going to be captain; that his intended choice was still dithering about whether he wanted to do it.

Warren had left a message. He wanted to know whether I would captain the World Cup squad. There was no turning back now. I didn't know whether they were still up picking the squad, so I decided to send a text message: 'Of course, I would like to be captain. It would be a huge honour.'

That was it. I was captain of Wales. And at twenty-two, their youngest ever World Cup captain.

At noon on Monday 22 August 2011, the WRU chairman David Pickering, with me sitting on his left and Warren on his right, announced the thirty-man squad that would go to New Zealand.

Martyn Williams wasn't in it. That was a real shock. I think if there had been one more place available he would have gone, but unfortunately he was the one to miss out. The measure of the man was that he immediately sent me a text congratulating me and wishing me good luck for the tournament. He has sent me a text before every international I've played in fact, and then always talked to me about the game afterwards.

Richard Hibbard was also extremely unfortunate. He injured his ankle in the second half of the Argentina match, and this just after he had returned from shoulder surgery. His place was taken by Ken Owens. Otherwise, there were few surprises.

'We've had a few injuries in the back three,' said Warren. 'And we wanted to make sure we had cover there. It needed bolstering up, so we went for 16–14. We told Andy Powell before the Argentina game, his game had to be error-free and he needed to take his opportunities, and he delivered. He played his way into the squad. You can only pick thirty. If we had gone for a 17–13 split, we would have taken two sevens. In such a tough group, there won't potentially be huge changes game to game, but we do have quality players we can call in. We don't often carry a specialist seven on the bench. I had a chat with Martyn in the week. He has been an unbelievable servant to Welsh rugby. He is selfless, a great servant. Gethin Jenkins [who had calf trouble] is unlikely to be fit for the South Africa game, although he should definitely be right for the Samoa match. He's an important quality player, which is why we are taking a bit of risk. We know how good he is.'

To the assembled press I said: 'I am delighted. To be a World Cup captain is one of the biggest achievements a rugby player could achieve. It's my first World Cup, so it will be new to me. I imagine it will be the same as other Test matches, just a bit more intense. We are positive. The players enjoy each other's company, and it is going to be a positive camp to be around. We are in a good place at the moment.'

And that is the way I felt. It was time to forget all the uncertainty and negativity about the captaincy. It was time to crack on. I wasn't going to try to act like a captain, I was just going to be myself. If something needed to be said, I would say it. But I wasn't going to talk just for the sake of talking. There would be plenty of senior players around me. They were not just senior players because they were older than many of us youngsters, but rather because they were experienced, consistent performers. It seemed they were all on my side. They wanted me to be captain, so it might not be so bad after all.

If I'm honest, the line of questioning from some sections of the press seemed a little bit negative. It was all about how young I was, as if they were questioning whether I could do the job. I know that I have been adding considerable fuel to that argument in the way I have been talking so far in this book, but they didn't know any of that then.

I quite like proving people wrong. When I was sixteen I remember watching the British and Irish Lions playing in New Zealand. I dreamed of wearing their No. 7 shirt one day, and so that Christmas I was given a Lions No. 7 shirt. I wore it everywhere. I would get quite emotional wearing it. But then I was told by one of the coaches at the Cardiff Blues that I would be a second row, not an openside flanker. I just thought: 'I'm not having this. No one is setting my boundaries for me. I'm going to play seven.' We had a training session that day. I finished that and went home, then trained again on my own for probably an hour and a half. It was probably the hardest session I had ever done in my life, but it was done for one reason and one reason alone: I would decide which position I played, and if people were still questioning that, I would make damned sure that I was in such good physical shape that I simply had to play there.

Maybe it was time to show that sort of attitude again regarding the captaincy. But just in case there were any lingering doubts, Andy had another good idea: to write a book. Not this book, but rather a collection of various reminders of who I am, where I came from, and who helped me to get to where I am, to use as an inspirational and motivational tool.

I called it 'Warby's Winning Ways'. It included a whole host of things, from my leadership compass to my personal identity statement, to photographs of me playing well, to quotes of approval from fellow players which I always set great store by (for instance Martyn saying that he thought I could be a British Lion), to positive press clippings (Andy sorted them out for me so that I did not have to trawl through any negative stuff), to the sponsorship deals I'd achieved. There was a list of my heroes, including the boxer Lennox Lewis, Andy McCann, my schoolteacher Gwyn Morris and my brother Ben. There were pictures of all my family, because this was as much for them as it was for me, but there was also one of Ben on his own.

Every game I have ever played has been for Ben. He was a good player himself, a winger or centre for Glamorgan Wanderers, Cross Keys, Bridgend and Merthyr (where he played alongside Ben Morgan who had come across from Gloucestershire in search of a regular place in a better standard of rugby and would go on to play for the Scarlets and then in 2011 for England). But injuries did for him and he became a physiotherapist. He did have a job with the Newport Gwent Dragons Academy, but in 2012 was promoted to the assistant physio's post with the main regional squad at Rodney Parade.

We are not identical twins (I am about three inches taller and a couple of stone heavier than Ben), but at school there were times when we swapped over in lessons and nobody noticed. We were always inseparable. We chose the same subjects at A level (chemistry, biology and PE) and spookily got the same grades (A, A, B). Some people thought we were a bit weird because we were so obsessed with our training. We would train at school lunchtimes, then at home on our multigym, and often in Caedelyn Park in Rhiwbina, where we would play one-on-one rugby, running at each other as hard as we could. It never hurt when you were ten – and we would really go for it – but the winner would feel sorry for the other guy because we got on so well. We were hugely competitive, but we never had a fight.

This book of 'Warby's Winning Ways' filled me with confidence. I didn't show it to anyone apart from Andy and my family, but at the time it was a hugely important psychological tool for me, helping me through my fears and doubts. Now, as I write in 2012, I rarely use it because the thought processes and feelings it encourages come naturally, but back then, just before the World Cup, it was exactly what I needed.

It was time to see if Warby could indeed win at the World Cup.

5

So Close

At the pre-match press conference in Wellington before our first match of the 2011 World Cup against South Africa, I was sitting alongside our coach Warren Gatland, when he suddenly said: 'There are three definite world-class players at the break-down in this tournament – David Pocock, Richie McCaw and Heinrich Brussow. I'd rate the guy next to me in that category as well. A lot of people have not seen Sam Warburton, but he will create an impact after a few games in this tournament.'

Crikey. Where had that come from? Warren had given me no indication he was going to say something like that. It was hugely flattering, but it did take me by surprise. I sat there looking confident, but in my mind I was thinking: 'No pressure then!'

I knew that I'd played reasonably well in the Six Nations that year, and my form had improved through the summer games against the Barbarians and the two England matches, but that was still a big statement.

I'd always idolised McCaw – Richie 'McCaw-some' as I used to call him. For my thirteenth birthday I'd been given an All Black shirt with his name on the back and, of course, the number seven. To be mentioned in the same sentence as him was remarkable. Warren had advised me to study his play a long time before, but I'd actually been studying him for some time already.

When I was about fifteen I would get up on a Saturday morning and sit in front of the television watching him play-ing for the Canterbury Crusaders in a Super 14 match. I would have my pen and paper ready and I would note down everything McCaw did in the game. There would be a series of headings: Turnovers, Tackles, Carries, Passes and Rucks Hit, and I would mark in Roman numerals each time he did some-thing that fitted in each category. Then in the afternoon I would play for the Cardiff Blues Under-16s. After the match we would be given a print-out of our own statistics for the game. I would rush home so that I could compare mine with McCaw's. It would read something like this: me – 8 tackles, 16 rucks, 8 carries and 0 turnovers; McCaw – 21 tackles, 40 rucks, 18 carries and 5 turnovers. I'd look at it and think: 'You've got a bit of a way to go here, mate.'

On the way over to the World Cup, Rhys Long, the team analyst, showed me a magazine in which there was an in-depth interview with McCaw. It was a fascinating article, especially when he talked about the pressures of expectation as captain of New Zealand. I just couldn't imagine how he coped with it.

I remember talking to some New Zealand fans during the tournament. The number seven is almost mythical in their country. It is everywhere, even on fashionable clothes. That obsession with the position was the reason why I think random people were shouting my name when I was going back late one night to the hotel with my parents. They were complimenting me on my play up until then and I said: 'Thanks very much, but you must think Richie is the best.'

Their response showed how tough the New Zealand people are on their rugby heroes. 'Yeah, but he hasn't won a World Cup yet,' they said. I was thinking: 'Flippin' heck, the bloke has just won his 100th cap, he's captained his country in well over sixty of those matches, everybody in the world looks up to him as the best, and yet his own people are still questioning him.' It actually impressed me in a way. Those are seriously high standards the Kiwis demand of their players.

Presumably his legendary status is now safe, as they won that World Cup in the end.

But here I was being compared to him by my own coach. The World Cup had really started now! Until then it had all been remarkably low-key as we prepared in Wellington. Even that press conference in which Warren said those very kind words was only half the size of a normal press conference back home for a Six Nations match.

My agent Derwyn Jones had said to me before I left that it

would not be anything like a Six Nations campaign in terms of the media glare and pressure. And he was right, because what we found was that everything was concentrated on the home team. This was New Zealand's World Cup and they were determined to win it. Every newspaper devoted front and back pages, and plenty more inside, to the New Zealand rugby team.

Not that we minded. And not that I necessarily believed Derwyn after the weekend I had had just before I left for the World Cup. It was certainly a taste of what the World Cup meant in Wales. I'd gone down to west Wales to stay in Rachel's parents' caravan near St David's. I love going down there and getting away from things, and I thought this would be a great opportunity to spend quality time with Rachel before I went on tour, as she was not coming out to New Zealand due to her accountancy exams.

The problem was that the word must have spread pretty quickly around the caravan park that the Wales captain was spending a few days there. On the first day, Friday, there were about three knocks at the caravan door asking for autographs. On the second day there must have been ten or eleven requests. And by late afternoon the woman in charge of the caravan park had come over and asked if it would be OK if I did one big signing session that night so that everyone could get their chance as apparently my presence had caused a bit of a stir.

We were going out for a meal that evening so I asked if we could do it on Sunday morning instead. About an hour before we had arranged to do it, I looked out of the caravan window and there were ten to fifteen people waiting already. By the time I went outside there was what looked like an army there, with their shirts, rugby balls, posters and books to be signed!

As I said before, I do not mind doing these sorts of things, but sometimes it can be a bit overwhelming, and in this instance I was really worried as to how Rachel felt about it. It was my last time with her before I went away for at least six weeks, we were supposed to be chilling out, and here I was spending as much time with people I didn't know as I was with her.

But as ever she was brilliant. I think she found it quite funny and ended up taking photos of the whole thing. And then at last we got some peace and quiet as we went to our favourite seaside spot of St Non's, where legend has it that Non gave birth to St David, the patron saint of Wales. It is so relaxing there; we just lay on a bench for about an hour listening to the sea. It was wonderful.

But the very next day it was time to go. Of course it was emotional. I had to say goodbye to Rachel as she went off to work that morning. We tried to be strong, but Rachel admitted to me later that she drove off and, as soon as she got around the corner and out of my sight, she pulled over and cried her eyes out.

My first memory of the New Zealand World Cup was seeing Jonah Lomu's house in Maupuia as we arrived in Wellington. It may have been his former house actually, but Warren was very quick to point it out to us. And just like the man, it is massive: a modern pad up on a hilltop. Lomu was a hero of mine and many others amongst the youngsters in the squad, and while we were out in New Zealand we read with concern the daily news of him being in an Auckland hospital because of complications with his transplanted kidney.

My second memory? On the bus to the hotel a room list was being read out and keys handed out. But for some reason full names, including middle names, were being used, and there were some surprises. We'd had no idea that we were being coached by Robin Currie McBryde. Or that our media communications manager was John Glenville Williams!

There was a warm welcome in Wellington. A number of Welsh fans, in their red shirts and Welsh costumes, greeted us at the airport, and quite a few turned up at our training ground in Porirua to watch one of our training sessions, where we mingled at pitchside afterwards for them to gather autographs and photographs. There was also an official Maori welcome by the Ngatitoa community in Porirua City Leisure Centre. Now that was not something I'd seen before.

I remember being in the Rydges Hotel, with its sweeping views of Wellington harbour, with Dan Lydiate when Warren came up to speak to me. He wanted to talk about the Maori welcome and what I should expect. More importantly he wanted to tell me what I had to do in response to the Maori greeting. I was captain after all; I was going to have to lead this.

Suddenly Warren turned into a Maori. His eyes bulged and

his tongue poked out as he pretended to have a spear in his hand and perform a Maori dance. Dan and I just burst out laughing. It was brilliant.

Warren laughed too, but then explained what I needed to do when the Maori warrior issued his challenge to me. He puts a fern on the floor, and Warren told me that, whatever I did, I had to keep eye contact with the warrior while I was picking up the fern. Not to do so is considered very offensive and the warrior is likely to attack you!

So we went to the function, and I am at the front of the Welsh contingent as this warrior comes around the corner, jabbing his spear or fighting staff, which I'm told is called a taiaha, and whistling and making the sort of aggressive noises you would expect from a Maori. He then performed his haka challenge before leaving the fern on the floor for me and tip-toeing backwards as if on hot coals. He pointed his taiaha at the fern and poked out his tongue. This was my cue. I had to pick up the fern to indicate that we as a group came in peace and we could then share food with the Maoris.

But I was really nervous. I didn't want to get this wrong. I knew how much it meant to the locals. The Welsh and the Maori are very similar, having our own language and identity, and sharing the same sort of love for rugby and farming. I was so mindful of Warren's words that I must never take my eyes off the warrior, but could I find the fern on the ground? Not at first I couldn't. I was still staring at the warrior, but in my mind I was thinking, 'Where's that fern?' I had visions of being jabbed by the warrior at any moment. But thankfully I suddenly felt the fern in my hand, lifted it up and had performed my task. The Maori challenge had been accepted, and the warrior turned and led us into the hall, or marae as it is called.

There the Maori group performed a haka in front of us, as well as singing their song. And, in a move which apparently went down really well with our hosts, we responded by singing the Welsh love song 'Lawr Ar Lan Y Mor', telling of how a couple met down by the sea. We'd been practising hard at this song, even though I'm not an enthusiastic singer. On the previous Wales tour of New Zealand in 2010, Robin McBryde had read a Welsh language poem in response to the Maori welcomes and had talked about the importance of the Welsh language and its parallels with Maori culture. This time it had been decided to sing this song. We'd probably had six choir practices before we did it, including one on the team bus after training. Craig Mitchell was choir master, with Alun Wyn Jones as his deputy, and the song began with a solo line from Robin, with other solo lines for Ken Owens, Jamie Roberts and Leigh Halfpenny in between the choruses.

Leigh's first performance in practice caused a bit of a stir. He's got a really good voice but I think it is fair to say that it is a little high-pitched, and, added to the fact that he really hung onto his notes, it took the boys a bit by surprise. So much so that quite a few of us started giggling when we first heard it. And, as is the way in all sporting teams, he got some stick for it. For the next few days he was being called Aled Jones, and whenever some of the boys passed him in the hotel you could hear strains of Jones's famous rendition of 'Walking in the Air'. I felt a little bit bad about that because Leigh was taking his singing very seriously, but it was only banter.

Although this was a real cultural occasion in Wellington, with everyone having to use the traditional Maori greeting, called the hongi, where you press your nose and forehead against the person you are greeting, it was also the occasion on which we were presented with our RWC 2011 caps by Bill Beaumont, the former England captain and now senior IRB official.

I've always thought that how you train as a team in the week leading up to a match does not necessarily correlate to how you then perform in the match itself, but it would have taken a brave man not to be a little concerned after our training session on the Tuesday before the South Africa match.

It was a defence session under Shaun Edwards, and it was one of the worst we have ever done. We were simply shocking. Players were missing tackles all over the place. I don't know how to explain it even now. Were we tired, jet-lagged or just not switched on? I don't know. But to say that Shaun was not impressed would be a huge understatement. I have never seen him so angry with us.

The funny thing is that for the next few days we trained well. I was hugely keyed up for this game. Even before Warren had made his comment about Pocock, McCaw and Brussow, I had been thinking a lot about Brussow and my battle with him in this game. I had never played against him before, but I had watched him against the British and Irish Lions in 2009 and he had been awesome.

'It's going to be an interesting one,' I told the press before-hand. 'I haven't played against him yet. In terms of breakdown play, he's incredibly effective in that area and it's a battle I'm looking forward to. It's going to be tough. I think he's one of the better players in the world at the breakdown at the moment.'

I knew how important my battle with him was. If I could keep him quiet we would have a good chance of winning the match. The South Africans pride themselves on their work at the contact area and I needed to send out a message that we would not be bullied there.

It was obvious how South Africa were going to play the game, the first between the countries in a World Cup. Not only did they select their most experienced side in history, with 815 caps (and it would have been more if Bakkies Botha had not been out with an Achilles tendon problem, to be replaced by Danie Rossouw), but they also picked five forwards on the bench, including two props and a hooker. 'They are going to take us on up front and try to dominate us physically,' said Warren.

He'd actually gone a bit further and said to the press: 'They don't play any rugby, they don't do anything. They're very good at what they do in terms of set piece and they put the ball up in the air, use the power runners effectively and they're a strong defensive side. We pretty much know what they're going to do. Morne Steyn kicks penalties and drop goals and they will play to their strengths because that's what they're good at doing and they're definitely a hard side to beat. The last three times we've played them there's been very little in the scores . . . and we've outscored them seven tries to six in the last three matches, so there hasn't been a heck of a lot between the teams. We're in pretty good shape. We can match them physically and that's the key to the battle.'

Warren was spot on. We were not worried that Wales had only beaten them once in twenty-five matches. It was talked about a lot, but I always say that such things are irrelevant to the modern-day player. We could match them physically. That was what shocked the South Africans, I think. That was what shocked the rugby world as a whole. There had always been this perception that we couldn't quite match the top teams physically. We were to – quite literally – smash that perception in this match. We were revved up, even if we could not select Gethin Jenkins, Ryan Jones or Stephen Jones because of injuries.

The breakdown was clearly going to be a huge talking point during the tournament, so it was no surprise when I was asked about it in Wellington. Do openside flankers test the referees? That was the question. Uh, yes, we do, I'm afraid. That is our job. 'I think you have to really. No openside flanker wouldn't try it,' I said. 'I think Richie (McCaw) is the best at sussing out the referees but it's just part and parcel of the game. I could play eighty minutes and pick out ten things where someone has done something illegal, but it goes on all the time constantly. I think it's something all the players, from 1 to 15, try and do on the pitch at some stage.'

I had mentioned to Andy McCann that it was one of my

big goals to get the better of Brussow, but it was only part of the grand plan because I was again being mindful of the advice of my old teacher Gwyn Morris: 'Aim really high.' I was aiming high in wanting to be player of the tournament. And in order to do that I had to win every personal battle. I had to beat Brussow.

I hope it doesn't sound arrogant to say that I wanted to be the player of the tournament, but that is my mindset going into any tournament. I can't see any other way of approaching it. I am not alone in thinking that way. Most of the younger guys in the Wales squad think the same. In our minds we were going to the World Cup to win it, or at the very least to reach the semi-finals. When George North and I were saying such things in the camp, I think it surprised a few of the older heads at first. They weren't used to such talk, but I think on reflection they found it really refreshing. They can help us youngsters in so many ways with their experience, but we can also help them with our youthful ambition and fearlessness.

I used that attitude in my speech to the team before the South Africa match. I was so pumped up. Each week during the World Cup, Andy would do a motivational video for me, with clips from the training in Poland through to my best bits from the warm-up games. It was set to the music of my favourite song, Anthrax's 'Refuse to be Denied', and it would include words such as 'professionalism', 'work ethic' and 'leadership' on the screen at various times. Every video would end with those words: REFUSE TO BE DENIED.

That is my motto. Before every game my dad will send me

a text and it will always finish with those same words in capital letters: REFUSE TO BE DENIED. If I did have a tattoo, that is what it would read. The only problem is that Rachel has always said she will finish with me if I ever have a tattoo – and she's serious! So I won't be having a tattoo.

Anyway, that video was on both my iPad and iPhone. On the morning of the game I did my 'mental primer' with Andy and then I went back to my room and watched it.

We went to the ground, the Wellington Regional Stadium, or, as everyone still calls it, the 'Cake Tin'. I had all my strapping done and we did the team warm-up outside. After we came back inside, I went into one of the toilet cubicles to watch the video again on my iPhone. I put on my headphones for the audio and turned up the volume.

'With my raised fist, yeah/Never be denied/I stand and resist again.' Out pumped the lyrics of 'Refuse to be Denied'. And at the end, up came the words on the screen: REFUSE TO BE DENIED.

I took off my headphones and I just couldn't wait to speak to the boys. So much for the bloke who didn't want to be captain and didn't want to speak to the team. Now I couldn't wait.

'People have written us off for this World Cup,' I said. 'People have said that we might not even be able to get out of this group. Others have talked about us getting to the quarter-finals. But even that's not enough. We can get to a semi-final. That's how good we are. Anything else will be a failure.'

As we walked out onto the 'Cake Tin' field, we got our first sighting of the Maori warrior issuing his challenge to both teams. One of them was at every game as the teams walked out, and it really made you realise that you were in New Zealand for the World Cup. It made you feel like you were going to war, and throughout the tournament it became my mental switch that this was now game time. I loved that moment, and from then on Andy would include it at the start of my motivational videos for each game.

We did go to war. It was a brutally physical game, as they always are against South Africa. But we lost 17–16. Did we deserve to lose? Probably not, but we did, and that is all that matters in international sport. I've spoken before about some Wales sides of yesteryear being too happy with heroic defeats, so I'm not about to start praising one too much here. And I did think immediately afterwards: 'Oh no, we're going to be seen to be just like some of those Wales teams of the past.'

But having said that, and even though it was galling to be so close and yet so far, I do think we made a statement that night in Wellington. It would obviously have been a much, much bigger statement to everyone else in the tournament had we won, but still I think the rugby world woke up to this Wales team that night.

Had there been much talk of Dan Lydiate and his low chop tackles before that night? What about Toby Faletau? He scored a try and showed that he will be a world-class No. 8 for years to come. For him, at just twenty years of age, to be playing in one of the most physical positions in the game, I thought it was unbelievable what a good performance he put in. Mike Phillips was brilliant; Jamie Roberts smashed into anyone and anything; Rhys Priestland was so calm at fly-half. The scrum was solid, the line-out went excellently, with only two lost from seventeen throws because of a fine performance from hooker Huw Bennett and superb efforts from the second rows Alun Wyn Jones and Luke Charteris. There were heroes all across the field for us. Yet we lost . . .

I look back on that game and I am still very proud of my own performance. I won the man-of-the-match award. That doesn't often happen to a player on the losing side.

I keep all my man-of-the-match awards in a glass cabinet in the back room of my house. This one from the South Africa match I keep in the front room on my lamp table. It is a special little trophy, designed by two Maori artists apparently and made in part with pounamu, which is a green stone that can only be found in New Zealand. I'm told it is bad luck to buy pounamu for yourself, so I bought Rachel and my mum a necklace made from it as presents from my time at the World Cup. I also bought a Maori wood carving each for my parents, Ben, Holly, and Rachel's parents Geoff and Sue, as well as one for me and Rachel that stands in our front room along with that man-of-the-match trophy.

Each trophy for the man of the match was made individually, with the wooden base inscribed with the latitude and longitude co-ordinates and contours to show the location of each match; in this case, Wellington. I am very proud of that trophy. I gave absolutely everything in that game, and it was my best game for Wales at the breakdown. I'd have swapped it for a Wales win, though.

I made twenty tackles in the match and six turnovers. Having said that I wanted to beat Brussow that day, I think I did. Again I hope that's not perceived as arrogance. That just the way I saw it. So too did those judging the man of the match. And South Africa's captain John Smit did say of me afterwards: 'He's a pain to play against. He is unbelievable at the breakdown, really busy and difficult to take care of. He will have some really good Test matches for Wales in the future and I am sure he is really going to stand out in this tournament.' Cheers, John! Everyone likes that sort of commendation from their fellow players, if they're totally honest.

I knew I was annoying the South Africans during the match. As it wore on I could hear them shouting more and more at each breakdown: 'Smash him. Get him off the ball!' There might have been the odd swear word in there too, but I don't want to upset my mum again by repeating them.

In their desire to get me off the ball they went a little too far on one occasion. I'll use Shaun Edwards's words, but they are certainly not ones with which I disagree.

'It was a cheap shot,' Shaun said after the game. 'It was a similar sort of action to what happened on the [2009] Lions tour – it was Bakkies Botha that time – with a shoulder charge on someone who was competing on the ball. If our captain, and our outstanding player on the day, had had to go off we would have been even more cheesed off than what we were.'

In private the coaches were even more miffed. They weren't happy about the incident at all, and it was a surprise that there was no citing concerning it.

Basically, I was at a ruck and I was taken out late as one of their players piled into the back of my head. I try never to lie on the floor with an injury because I don't want to show the opposition that I am hurt. That is the same mentality we were fostering amongst the squad during our trips to Poland. No one was ever allowed to put their hands on their knees when they were tired. It was a massive theme throughout both camps out there: never show anyone you are tired.

So I tried to do the same here and not show the South Africans that I was hurt, but the truth was that I was struggling. It was one hell of a blow. I was rubbing the back of my head; I was surprised I could locate it because my head was spinning that much. But I do remember thinking, 'Don't let it put you off "jackaling". That's what they want. Keep frustrating them.' So at the next breakdown I competed like mad just to annoy them, to make sure they knew that they hadn't won their little battle to get rid of me. I was still going to be there at that breakdown, and the next. And the next.

That was not the most controversial incident of the night, though. We had had a bad start when Francois Steyn had scored as early as the third minute, creeping in at the corner after Jacques Fourie had made the initial break, with Morne Steyn converting from the touchline. We were 7–0 down.

But there was no panic. James Hook kicked a penalty, and then in the fourteenth minute we were awarded another penalty after JP Pietersen made a high tackle on Mike Phillips. I'm always one for taking the three points on offer in a Test match, because you see sides going for the corner so many times and it not paying off. And as we knew this was always going to be a tight arm-wrestle, I had no hesitation in asking Hooky to kick at goal once again. He lined it up from the left-hand side of the field and about 40 metres out, and, from where I was in the middle of the field, it looked as if he had struck it pretty well.

Well enough and accurately enough to go over? I couldn't tell from where I was. It certainly went high in the air. And that was the problem. It went so high that it went above the line of the posts and looked as if it curved from right to left late in its flight. Had it curved in enough to go inside the invisible line of the right-hand post, as Hooky looked and kicked at it? Hooky thought so, and turned away and began to run back as if it had gone over.

But the touch judges' flags stayed down. The Irishman George Clancy and the Kiwi Vinny Munro did not think the ball had gone over. The referee that day was the Englishman Wayne Barnes. Hooky asked him to go to the television match official to check that the touch judges' adjudication was correct, but Barnes declined to do so.

Should I, as captain, have got involved? Probably. Warren asked afterwards whether I had spoken to Barnes about it, and I admitted that I hadn't. A bit like the Barbarians game and my first time in charge, I had shown some inexperience. If I'm honest, it did not even cross my mind to talk to him. But naturally I felt bad about it afterwards. I suppose that you have to go through these experiences as captain to learn from them. Having said that, having watched the video it is very difficult to say for certain whether it went over. Even if Barnes had asked the TMO for a decision, he may not have been able to give a conclusive verdict.

And it is easy to look back now and say we were robbed of three points that would have given us victory. But even if that penalty had been given, it might have changed the mindset of the South Africans. They could still have come back. It was in the first half, remember, and there were still sixty-odd minutes to go, so we can't just blame the loss on that incident. It's impossible to say what might have happened afterwards.

Hooky and Morne Steyn each kicked a penalty so that we were 10–6 down at half-time. And we were buoyed by the loss of their second row, Victor Matfield, after forty-three minutes with a hamstring strain. With half an hour to go Hooky kicked another penalty after a massive surge from Jamie Roberts. It was 10–9.

Three minutes later we were ahead, after scoring a try through Toby. First Dan Lydiate had made good ground, then Rhys Priestland popped to Toby, who went over despite going to ground just before the line (but not being held) and then diving under Frans Steyn. Video confirmation was asked for, but there was no real doubt, and when Hooky converted it was 16–10 to us.

There were twenty-five minutes to go. We nearly scored again when Toby made a stunning 20-metre break and Jamie Roberts took the ball on, but sadly it was lost near the line.

We knew that South Africa would rally, and they did just that. After a period of concerted pressure they eventually scored when scrum-half Fourie du Preez popped up a pass to replacement winger Francois Houggard to score under the posts.

It was a disappointing score to concede. Houggard ran a clever shadow line behind Du Preez, but defending that is something we do all the time in training. With the way our blitz defence is organised you need to jam in tight alongside the scrum-half in that instance. We didn't quite do that there and the gap opened up for Houggard, which he took gladly. Morne Steyn converted and South Africa were back in front.

There were still fourteen minutes left, though, and we had our chances to score. Indeed, just a couple of minutes later we managed to secure a good position from which Rhys Priestland had a drop-goal attempt. Unfortunately his kick went to the left of the posts and poor Rhys was left with his head in his hands. Not that I am blaming him. As I said about the contentious penalty from Hooky, so much could have happened after that.

And it did, with Hooky having a difficult penalty chance from out on the right. He missed it, sadly, but when he said afterwards, 'The wind changed direction two or three times while I was lining it up. It was blowing all over the place,' he was not making idle excuses. It must be a kicker's nightmare to play in that stadium. It is one hell of a windy place (it's not known as 'windy Wellington' for nothing), and I don't blame Rhys or James for nudging those kicks wide. They were really tough kicks.

That was it then. We'd lost. As Warren said: 'In the end we were not good enough. To get 60 per cent of territory and possession against South Africa is a massive step in terms of where we have come as a team, but at the end of the day we weren't quite clinical enough and South Africa won. We created some good opportunities and you have to take them at this level. I was really impressed by the players. A number of them took responsibility for the loss, and from an individual point of view that was pleasing. The penalty was one of those things that happen in sport. It was a tough game for Wayne Barnes to officiate and not many of his decisions affected the game. I do not want to say anything negative about him because we have him later on in the tournament against Fiji.

'We believed we were good enough to beat South Africa. We were accused of talking ourselves up, but we absolutely believed we could win. When you look at the statistics, we had more territory and possession and put ourselves in a position to get the victory. We have to move on and focus on Samoa. They will be tough, but we have to be confident.'

Ah, yes, it was Samoa next. That was always going to be tough. But we had made a point. The World Cup is the ultimate opportunity to prove oneself, and, despite the loss, I think we had all proved ourselves in Wellington.

We would be marked men from now on, but that did not concern us. It was the belief of all the players that we would rather have the tag of being expected to win and people wanting to chase you, than being the underdog.

Those days were gone.

6

Out of the Pool of Death

The game against Samoa was to be in Hamilton, Warren Gatland's hometown, but we did not go there immediately from Wellington. During our journey from the southernmost tip of New Zealand's north island up to Hamilton, we went to the middle of that island and stayed near Lake Taupo for five nights.

It was a wonderful experience. We stayed in apartments and ate some exceptional local food, and we really took in the New Zealand culture in a relaxed environment. There was another Maori welcome for us, this time in Hatepe. I was a little bit better at picking up the fern this time. But there was a moment of humour, which I hope in relating I am not disrespecting the Maori culture.

We were waiting at the end of the road for the Maori warrior to appear, and I was up at the front, as I had to be as captain. Alongside me was Dan Baugh. There was a real sense of excitement. It was almost as if we were going to war, just as we had against South Africa in Wellington. I turned to Dan and said: 'If I get anything wrong here and the warrior starts whipping me with his stick, you jump in and help me, right?'

Dan nodded and laughed. And then suddenly the warrior appeared. He was a monster of a man! I was sure he was Jonah Lomu in disguise. Just as I was taking this in, Dan leant across and whispered to me: 'He's all yours. I'm not going anywhere near him!'

I wanted to burst out laughing, but of course I couldn't. As it turned out, the warrior was a lovely bloke. He introduced us to his tribe and we enjoyed another excellent cultural experience. We sang again, which went down well again, and Robin McBryde presented them with a Welsh love spoon and explained the meaning behind it.

George North, as the youngest member of the tour party, had been given the responsibility of looking after a two-foot-long love spoon throughout the trip, and he was supposed to do the explaining, but he is a little bit nervous about that sort of thing, so he handed the job over to Robin. George had enough problems looking after the love spoon anyway. It has been a tradition for a while that the spoon is always taken to official functions, but it also seems to be a tradition that the boys try to steal it from its guardian so that he incurs a fine.

Sure enough, George lost the spoon. I think some of the boys got hold of the master key in one of the hotels and sneaked into his room to steal it. I have never seen George so stressed. As he later admitted: 'Ninety-two hours later – and about twelve room raids – I finally found it in Adam Jones's room. It cost me three figures in fines and the boys wound me up. I wasn't happy. It kept changing hands and I was always just behind it.'

After every game we presented the opposition with a specially made love spoon. But when we played South Africa in that first game they did not have anything to swap with us, so we didn't present it to them. Alan Phillips said to me: 'Do you want to keep the love spoon?' I said yes without any hesitation, and it is in my kitchen at home now. I've always fancied having a love spoon in the kitchen because it is a great representation of one's Welshness. This one has got a daffodil and a dragon on it, as well as a protea, the national flower of South Africa. On the back it says: 'Wales v South Africa 11 September 2011 Rugby World Cup'. It is a nice memento.

Up in Taupo we then had the most enormous feast. We really did relax up there. Staying in apartments helped. I was sharing with Dan Lydiate and Ryan Jones, and one night we decided to have a movie night. We invited Toby Faletau too for a night in for the back-rowers. First we took a taxi to the local supermarket where we stocked up on sweets, chocolate and popcorn. Then back at the apartment we pushed the sofas together, put on our PJs and laid back while Ryan sorted out the film from the extensive collection on his iPad.

We also had a nice open training session at Owen Delany Park, where loads of Welsh fans turned up. Then one day after training we were taken to the DeBretts thermal spa resort to do our warm-downs and recovery work. Unfortunately, there was an added attraction there that naturally pulled some of the boys towards it: some huge water slides. But the problem was that the bus was waiting to take us back to our accommodation. The next thing there was a huge splash as somebody came down one of the slides. We all looked round to see the identity of the head that was about to pop out of the water. If we were honest, we knew who it was going to be. Yes, it was Andy Powell! That was it. We were all in. All of a sudden there was a huge queue at the top of the slides. This was fun time, and the bus was told to wait.

But by Saturday it was time to get serious again. It was time to go to Hamilton for the Samoa match on the Sunday. We were pleasantly surprised when we arrived at the hotel. There were a lot of people milling around outside and quite a few TV cameras. Our performance against South Africa had obviously woken everyone up in New Zealand. They were here to see us. Fantastic.

We walked into the hotel foyer – and guess who was there? Yes, the New Zealand team. They had hammered Japan the night before – 83–7 with thirteen tries – and they were just moving on. All the attention was on them, not us. Our egos left with the Kiwis, I think. Oh well.

In fairness we received good support in Hamilton, mainly because of Warren's connection. He was born in Hamilton and played 140 matches for Waikato, and also coached them to the Air New Zealand Cup in 2006. We played both Samoa and Fiji in Hamilton, and Warren said beforehand: 'Samoa are going to have a lot of support, as will Fiji when we come back to play them in the final game of our pool, but we are hoping some of the Waikato people will be getting behind Wales as well. We played here on our summer tour of New Zealand last year and I told all of the players what to expect then. We all really enjoyed the experience and the welcome we had in Hamilton. It is a special atmosphere on match day. It will be very much like coming home for me and we are hoping all the locals bring their Mooloo Bells and ring them for Wales!'

Losing to South Africa meant we simply had to beat Samoa now. We were under pressure, but, as I quoted to the press at the time, Alun Wyn Jones always says we are a much better team under pressure. Inevitably there was lots of talk about the fact that Wales had lost to Samoa on both occasions they had met in World Cups, in 1991 and 1999. I'd played against them in Cardiff in 2009 when we'd only won 17–13, but, as I mentioned earlier, all these historical statistics were irrelevant to us.

In 1991 Wales lost 16–13 in Cardiff on 6 October, the day after my third birthday; I don't remember my celebrations being soured. George North wasn't even born! In 1999 Samoa won 38–31 in Cardiff, nine days after my eleventh birthday. Again I don't think it scarred me.

I said much of this to the press in Hamilton: 'I don't think the players are taking notice of what has happened in the

119

past . . . It's all irrelevant. The squad is a lot different now. They have some big ball-carriers, so we know it is going to be a big physical challenge.'

Indeed it was. Samoa had beaten Australia 32–23 in Sydney in July, even though they had lost to Tonga and Fiji in the previous eight days. And they had begun their World Cup by beating Namibia 49–12 in Rotorua.

The build-up to the match was overshadowed by terrible news from back home in Wales. On the Thursday before the match we had heard that there had been an accident at the Gleision Colliery, a drift mine in the Swansea valley, in which four miners had died. They were named as Charles Breslin, 62; David Powell, 50; Garry Jenkins, 39; and Philip Hill, 44. It was horrible news, and we asked the authorities if we could observe a minute's silence before the match, but it was not possible. We did, however, wear black armbands for the match.

The day before the Samoa game, Ireland were playing Australia in Auckland. I was sharing a room with Jon Davies at the time, and we watched the game together. When the final whistle went we just looked at each other and grinned. Ireland had won 15–6. Australia had been without David Pocock and he is a huge player for them – not many teams can handle him at the breakdown – but this was a result we hadn't reckoned with. It had suddenly thrown the tournament wide open. Maybe that South Africa defeat was a blessing after all.

Ireland were probably going to win their group, which meant that if we could see off Samoa, Fiji and Namibia, we would be playing them rather than Australia in the quarter-final. No disrespect to Ireland, but we thought that we could beat them. In fact we knew we could because we had beaten them in our last encounter in the Six Nations. I passed Rob Howley at breakfast the next morning and we both smiled. 'Did you see the game last night?' he asked. He knew the answer already because I was smirking. No one was saying it, but I reckon most of us were thinking it: 'We can get to a semi-final here.' We were on the cusp of something special.

But first we had to beat Samoa. We were unchanged from the South Africa match, at least in the starting line-up. There was a significant change on the bench, however, where Gethin Jenkins was brought in. Because of toe and calf problems, he hadn't played at all since appearing for Cardiff Blues in early January, and hadn't played for Wales since the meeting with the All Blacks at the Millennium Stadium in November 2010.

And we did win, by the margin of seventeen points to ten, after an immensely tough struggle. I immediately thought of the four miners. 'I would like to dedicate the win today to the families of the miners back home,' I said on the pitch afterwards. 'Our thoughts are with them.'

Without a doubt it was the dirtiest game I have ever played in. One of their players kicked me flush on the chin, Dan Lydiate injured his ankle when he was hit by some kind of UFC (Ultimate Fighting Championship) move and went down, and then his replacement Andy Powell was cleaned out by a head butt that sent him flying. It was vicious. And I know Warren wasn't happy about it.

We had to make 147 tackles as a team, with Toby Faletau

making 29 of them, Andy Powell 28 and Luke Charteris 18 (I think I made 15). Those are some staggering figures, and they don't show what a good match Alun Wyn Jones had. He was immense and deservedly won the man-of-the-match award.

We were 10–6 down at half-time and needed a 67th-minute try from Shane Williams to seal victory, but you know what? I never thought we were going to lose. The players had talked passionately about not losing at half-time, and you could just tell in the second half that we were playing at a pace that was eventually going to be too much for Samoa. You just get that feeling on a rugby field sometimes, and even when Shane scored I did not celebrate that much, because I knew it was coming. I thought from that moment on we closed the game out pretty comfortably. The result was never in doubt.

Our scrummage had gone really well in the first half, but we had lost Dan after just nine minutes, and at the end of that half we found ourselves under real pressure. Firstly Maurie Faasavalu thought he had scored, but was penalised for a double movement by referee Alain Rolland, and then eventually prop Anthony Perenise scored out on the left. But, just as we hadn't when conceding an early try to South Africa in Wellington, we did not panic. We knew that we had the fitness levels to stretch Samoa over the full eighty minutes. We just wanted to keep the ball in play as much as we could and back our fitness levels towards the end of the match. That had probably been the reason why we had tried to play a little bit too much rugby in our own half in the first half. We had put ourselves under too much pressure at times.

Leigh Halfpenny arrived for the second half in place of the injured James Hook, who had kicked our two penalties up until then, but had hurt his shoulder. Rhys Priestland took over the kicking duties and landed two penalties, the first off the crossbar, so that we were leading 12–10 after sixty-five minutes.

Leigh looked good immediately. He had a fine half, I thought, and was not the only replacement to make a strong impact. Bradley Davies and Lloyd Burns both did well, as did Gethin after his long lay-off. He put in a couple of huge hits after coming on in the last quarter, as well as a couple of vital turnovers. Leigh made the important break for Shane's try, after taking an up-and-under and brilliantly wriggling free off the floor to run 50 metres before feeding Jon Davies, whose overhead pass eventually found Shane on the bounce.

It was actually Shane's 55th Test try, but I just said afterwards: 'Leigh came on and added some great momentum to the side and Shane finished it off as we've seen him do a million times before. If our backs get a sniff they're pretty handy.'

Every contact was brutal, but in the past everybody would have been talking about huge hits by the islanders on us. This time there were some huge hits by us on the Samoans. There was one early on by Jamie Roberts on Seilala Mapusua, and then another when George North bumped off Tasesa Lavea spectacularly.

I remember being happy with a steal off Alesana Tuilagi late on in the game, but paying for it as I was smashed. I always set myself the target of at least four turnovers in a match, and at this stage I was still only on three. Tuilagi was careering down the touchline and somebody else – I can't remember who – made a good tackle on him. I went in as the 'plus one' as we call him and managed to turn the ball over. I gave the ball to Phillsy and we cleared the danger. All the boys were tapping me on the head to say well done, but I so wanted to say to them: 'Stop hitting my head! It's killing me!' I had been smashed all day at the breakdown. It was such a tough game that the next day I emailed my sponsor, Adidas, about the possibility of sending me a head guard.

But we'd won. That was all that really mattered. As Warren said: 'I thought we showed some great character. We knew today that Samoa was a must-win game. I said forget about the performance, we just knew we had to win. We're not that happy with the performance, but we're very happy with the result. A few years ago, or twelve months earlier, we might not have won that game. Our whole World Cup was about going out in that second half and digging deep. And they did that. I thought our conditioning was great. The longer the game went on, the stronger and fitter we looked.'

I think we gave Warren the birthday present he wanted. It had been his 48th the day before the game, and it was nice of the World Cup organisers to arrange the schedule so that we arrived in his home town on his birthday! We sang Happy Birthday to him and presented him with a cake. 'Speech!' everyone shouted at him. 'Just give me a win tomorrow,' he said. Fair enough.

Without being rude or disrespectful to Warren or his hometown, Hamilton is a fairly quiet place. As our next game against Namibia in New Plymouth wasn't until the following Monday – a rare eight-day turnaround which gave our battered bodies time to recover – we stayed there until the Friday after the match, which had been on the Sunday. The Monday was a complete day off, so we went wandering around Hamilton. George North found a remarkable little place. It was called the Cheesecake Shop and they did the most phenomenal cheesecakes. They tasted all the better because George bought one for me and Andy McCann! We still talk about those cheesecakes now. When you have to be so strict about your diet for so much of the time, it makes little treats all the more memorable.

The break also gave us time to go surfing. I went to Raglan Bay, west of Hamilton and famous for its tremendous surf, with Leigh Halfpenny, Lloyd Williams and Scott Williams. It was a tremendous experience, but I have to say that Leigh and I were hopeless. I'd never tried it before, but was glad I did. You could see Lloyd knew what he was doing. He's from Cowbridge, which is closer to the sea than Rhiwbina!

After the surfing we went on a luxury boat where we had a marvellous barbecue. It was great to chill out and relax. In fairness Warren made sure that we did relax at the right times, and he also made sure that we saw plenty of the country. He always says that you have to be able to switch on and then switch off at the appropriate times.

Before the trip there were all sorts of different committees appointed, for food, laundry and just general discipline, where fines were issued for all manner of things, from wearing the wrong socks at training to having a pair of trousers that were deemed terrible! By the end of the trip we had gathered about £2000 in the kitty, which we used for various purposes including charity donations, as well as paying for some drinks for the players after the third-place play-off match against Australia.

We also had an entertainments committee comprising Jamie Roberts, Huw Bennett and Jon Davies, and for days off they would put up a clipboard in the team room with a variety of trips to choose from. There was a helicopter ride in Wellington, as well as a visit to a karting centre. There was fishing and jet boating on Lake Taupo, and some boys played golf if their shoulders weren't too bad after a game. And later in the tournament some of us went quad biking in Woodhill Forest outside Auckland. The course we went on was amazing. It was so scenic. At first we were among pine trees on a forest dirt track, where there were lots of good jumps. Then we went over some sand dunes, before going along the stunning beach of Muriwai, where we could get up to 30 or 40mph on the bikes.

Of course, boys being boys, everyone got a bit cocky. Toby Faletau started doing 'donuts' (spins) in front of the boys on the beach and ended up falling off, with the rest of us having to pull his bike off him. He was suitably embarrassed. There was quite a big group of us doing it, including the popular team photographer Ben Evans, who has taken over from his father Huw in recent years. He's only very slight in build though, and he struggled to handle the big bike. He ended up crashing into a tree and breaking his bike. I think he hurt himself too, banging his head against the tree!

Before that we were haring through the forest – there was George North, Toby and Dan Lydiate (who has a quad on his family farm near Llandrindod Wells and so knew how to handle one) at the front, and I was behind them with Alun Wyn Jones, Ben and Huw Bennett. Alun Wyn Jones suddenly sped off and so I chased him. He was standing up and waving at me when suddenly he saw a tree up ahead.

He had two options: the easier path, which was to the left and quite smooth, or the much harder one to the right, which would involve a jump. He panicked. He was going so fast that he then had no time to do either. You could see the fear on his face as he braced himself for the inevitable crash. He even tried to use the brake, but used the accelerator instead, so all you could hear was this extra revving as he hit the tree and slid down, just like they do in cartoons. He was lying on the floor with his bike on top of him, its wheels still spinning.

Now I was panicking. It had looked like a scene from that TV show, *Jackass*. It didn't look good. We didn't really want to be losing our main man in the second row through a quad-biking accident. All sorts of things went through my mind at that moment, not least what the press might make of it. We could suddenly be attracting similar headlines to England, given all the stick they'd had for their off-field activities during this World Cup, although I don't think this was in the same category of danger as the bungee jumping for which they had been criticised. And we hadn't been out on a bender in a local bar either. Not that we'd all been behaving like monks, as Warren was keen to point out when the attention was focused on England and we were being held up as the polar opposites.

But nonetheless I was worried. I skidded to a halt. 'Are you OK, Al?' I shouted. He looked up and smiled. Thank God for that. He was OK. I wasn't hanging around for him now, and off I went, laughing uncontrollably. I was still laughing when I caught up with the rest of the boys. It was one of the funniest things I'd seen, mainly because Al had been so cocky on the bike just beforehand!

I wouldn't have been able to go quad biking in Hamilton after the Samoa game, though. I was struggling. I had hurt my knee during the game and it was seriously painful with a lot of swelling. Sadly it was the start of a long period of trouble with that knee.

The only training session I did before the Namibia match was the team run the day before the game. Otherwise I just rested up and iced my knee. Not that I could let it be known how bad it was. I even pretended to warm up before one session – when the cameras are allowed in for the first ten minutes – even though I could barely run, let alone sprint, because my knee was so full of fluid. After we had played Namibia we returned to Hamilton to play Fiji and I got an MRI scan on it, which showed that I had a Baker's cyst at the back of the knee, and it had burst.

So after the Samoa game in Hamilton I missed the open training session out at Waitomo in the farming area outside

Hamilton. Apparently there were about 700 people there, including lots of schoolchildren, with one group from Te Kuiti which is the hometown of the legendary Sir Colin Meads.

And after that the squad went to the Waitomo Glow-worm Caves, where they were given another Maori welcome by the guides there. They sang a traditional Maori song and the squad responded with 'Lawr Ar Lan Y Mor' and, this time, with 'Calon Lan' too. It was a really good visit apparently.

I stayed at the hotel to ice my knee, along with Dan who was icing his ankle. That lunchtime we decided to go out for lunch with the physio Prav Mathema and James Hook, who was also injured. We found a nice-looking brasserie-type place on the strip there in Hamilton. Prav came up with the idea of playing credit card roulette to see who paid for the meal. It was something the Scarlets boys, especially Jon Davies and Rhys Priestland, liked doing on tour. There was one meal in the Wagamama restaurant in Wellington where there were about eight of them, and Ken Owens lost the roulette and had to pay a huge bill. Basically, all the credit cards are put into a glass in the middle of the table and the waitress picks out one at a time, and the owner of the last one remaining has to pay for the meal. If your card is picked out before the end you must not celebrate. If you do, you have to pay. Nobody celebrated prematurely here. And it was Dan's card that came out last. Ha! I'm laughing now as I write that, because, as I mentioned before, he is a little bit tight when it comes to his money. He was devastated.

The day before I had been with Andy McCann and Ryan

Jones to watch a film, *The Change-Up*, an American comedy starring Ryan Reynolds and Jason Bateman, who play Mitch Planko and Dave Lockwood. Dave is a married lawyer with three children; Mitch is a bit of a down-and-out but he lives a stress-free life. One night after a few too many drinks they pee into a wishing fountain and wish that they had each other's lives. And that, of course, is what happens. But Dave misses his kids terribly, and that made Ryan, a father himself, feel sad. I know Dan Baugh also watched that film around the same time, and it made him miss home too.

Want to know why I know so much about this film? Because I watched it twice in the same day. I find it hard to say no sometimes, and after watching the film the first time, I went with George North and Leigh Halfpenny to the shopping mall. There was a cinema there. 'Let's watch *The Change-Up*,' they said. OK then ... It was a good film, and I had had enough of icing my knee for the day.

Dan was really struggling with his ankle. He wouldn't tell me how bad it was, because I think he'd been told not to tell any of the players. But subsequently it has emerged that the medical staff thought he would have to go home straight away, because it was so serious.

I could tell his head had gone, though. And not because of the credit card roulette. He was gutted. His girlfriend Nia and his parents had come out to New Zealand for two weeks, and unfortunately during the time they were there he didn't play a game.

But he meant so much to the team that he was given extra

time to prove his fitness. As Warren said: 'The initial verdict from the medics was that we were probably going to have to send him home because it was going to be a lot more serious. We decided to give him seventy-two hours or a bit longer to see if there was a big improvement in his ankle and there was.'

That it did improve was all down to Dan's professionalism. He gave it everything. He was getting up every two hours throughout the night to ice his leg, and every time I went into the physio room he was there having treatment of some kind. I'll give you Warren's wise words again: 'He has been so professional in the way he has rehabbed himself – you have to take your hat off to the young man. Dan is the type of character we want to build in this squad. He epitomises it. He missed training on Wednesday, coming to me and asking if I minded. Dan said he hadn't slept in the past seventy-two hours. He had been getting up every two hours and icing his leg.'

All the players were desperately hoping that he would be OK. It was the reason why I played against Namibia. In an ideal world, with my bad knee, I would have been given that game off, but we all had to play, and we all had to pray that none of us got injured (or in my case got injured more).

I said to the press: 'I put my feet up for a couple of days [after Samoa], had a bit of ice, and it's OK now. I want to play every game. I've had a few injuries in my career, and this is the best spell I have had so far fitness-wise. Warren said to the players: "You never know which game is your last Test for Wales." Every opportunity I have to play for Wales, I will take it with both hands.'

And I really mean that. I want to play in every Test because you never know when your last Test might be. But if any of us had got injured then, Dan would have been going home. We'd have only had three fit back-rowers. And you have to remember that Ryan Jones had been struggling with his calf. About a week before there had been talk about him going home too, which would have been desperately disappointing for him after he had missed the 2007 World Cup with a shoulder problem.

Thankfully Ryan was able to play a full eighty minutes against Namibia, remarkably his first appearance in a World Cup, and none of us did get injured in that match (I was taken off after just forty-eight minutes to be replaced by Andy Powell) or in the one against Fiji that followed, so that Dan was able to come back for the quarter-final. But it was a serious concern at the time.

New Plymouth was an interesting trip, mainly because I was sharing with Bradley Davies for the three nights we were there. Bradley is a real character, a 'beauty', as we say. There is always fun to be had when he is around. As soon as we got there he texted his Cardiff Blues second-row partner Paul Tito, who is from New Plymouth. 'New Plymouth is a s***hole,' he wrote. 'I can see why you came to Cardiff!'

A little harsh, I feel. But he was only joking. New Plymouth is quiet, yes, but we were a little unfortunate in that we were not in one of the best hotels. There was some sort of rankings system for this during the World Cup, and on that occasion it went against us. However, the beaches there are beautiful, as we discovered when we went to one of them for a warm-down and recovery after training one day.

And just as beautiful is the New Plymouth ground, the Yarrow Stadium, with the snow-capped volcano Mount Taranaki visible from it. We made eleven changes for the match there against Namibia. Of the backs only Jon Davies remained from the starting line-up against Samoa. Lee Byrne, Leigh Halfpenny, Aled Brew, Scott Williams, Stephen Jones and Tavis Knoyle all came into the starting side. Shane Williams, who had a bit of thigh problem after the Samoa match, Jamie Roberts and Mike Phillips were all rested, while James Hook was out injured, and George North and Rhys Priestland were on the bench.

Gethin Jenkins, Lloyd Burns and Craig Mitchell made up a new front row, Bradley came in at second row and Ryan Jones at blindside. And on the bench was hooker Ken Owens, who would come on to make his debut.

Of course, the big story was that this was to be Stephen Jones's 101st cap, making him Wales's most capped player, ahead of Gareth Thomas on 100. After that false start back at Twickenham in the first warm-up match of the summer, when he'd pulled out at the last minute, he was at last going to get what he thoroughly deserved. Quite rightly he led the side out.

We won 81–7, scoring twelve tries. And we got the bonus point we wanted. We would have been disappointed with anything less. Namibia had conceded 185 points in their three games before facing us, and had only had a four-day turnaround after being hammered 87–0 by South Africa in Auckland.

I think Namibia missed more tackles (42) than we made (38), so that tells you everything you need to know about the one-sidedness of the game. But that's not to say they weren't physical. They were!

They did trouble us at the contact area. And even though we raced into a 22–0 lead after seventeen minutes, we didn't score again in the first half, and the coaches were not happy at half-time.

But we sharpened up in the second half, scoring nine tries and fifty-nine points. Scott Williams scored a hat-trick and Stephen Jones celebrated his milestone by kicking six conversions and a penalty for a fifteen-point haul. I actually regret that one penalty he kicked now. It was early on, after just two minutes, and it was my decision that he should kick for goal. I know I've said before that I always look to take those points, but this was slightly different. With all due respect to Namibia we didn't really need to take that penalty. We should have kicked for the corner. 'Are you sure?' asked Stephen when I told him. I said: 'I want to give them respect. Let's build a lead first.'

'Whatever you say, Warbs,' Stephen laughed. 'You're the captain!' And I laughed back. I just should have been more ruthless.

Other tries came from Aled Brew, Toby Faletau, Gethin Jenkins, George North (2), Jon Davies, Lloyd Williams (with his first international try), Lee Byrne and Alun Wyn Jones. Rhys Priestland came on and also kicked three conversions.

Scott Williams's first try, after just seven minutes, was superb, with some lovely back play down the left after Jon Davies had given a deft inside pass to Leigh Halfpenny, but the try of the match was surely Gethin Jenkins's. From a quick line-out he found himself in midfield and from 35 metres out he took the ball, cutting back on an angle before darting and swerving like the back he always wants to be. Not a bad effort in his first start in any match since January (it was now September).

Then it was back to Hamilton for our final Pool D match against Fiji. By now half of New Zealand seemed to be on our side. The whole England story had blown up and we had a lot of locals coming up to us in the streets saying that they wanted a New Zealand v Wales final. It seemed that we had become everyone's second favourite team. We were playing a brand of rugby they liked to see.

We had a really good Welsh following in Hamilton too. The bars seemed to be full of fans in their red shirts, so one night during the week we decided to pop over to the bar on a corner opposite the hotel to mingle with some of them. You should have seen the looks on the fans' faces as we walked in! It was brilliant PR. We stayed there for a while, signing autographs and having our photographs taken, and everyone went home happy.

We made seven changes for the match, with George North, Jamie Roberts, Rhys Priestland, Mike Phillips, Adam Jones, Huw Bennett and Luke Charteris all returning to the starting side. Shane Williams was not risked because of his thigh injury, although he might have played had the opposition been more dangerous; James Hook and Dan Lydiate were still obviously out of contention. I was making my fourth successive start. Only Toby Faletau was doing the same.

Again there was history being raised before the game, with talk of Wales's shock 38–34 defeat by Fiji in the 2007 World Cup. Again it did not matter to us. We were a different side, with a different mindset.

We won 66–0, scoring nine tries. It was probably our best game of the tournament from a team perspective. Every off-load worked, every running line was spot on, every pass stuck. It was just one of those days. George North was unbelievably good, and I got my first World Cup try thanks to him, as he burst up the middle from what looked at first like a scrappy line-out, slicing the defence apart and then passing left over his shoulder to me. I only had to outstrip the one man covering across. That was our fourth try, and with it came a bonus point and also the knowledge that we were in the quarter-finals.

We had scored as early as the sixth minute when I snaffled a loose line-out and Jamie Roberts went charging over. The procession began. Scott Williams scored next, as lovely hands from Jamie fed a galloping George, before Scott was put away. George then deservedly got on the score sheet himself, after good work from Jamie and Huw Bennett, and Toby had been involved too. With Rhys Priestland converting all four first-half tries, as well as kicking a penalty, it was 31–0 at half-time.

We had spoken about not taking our feet off the pedal, and

My fiancée Rachel and I in our back garden before a charity dinner for the Velindre Cancer Centre for whom I am a patron.

I took this myself of my parents at the top of the Auckland Sky Tower after the disappointment of the semi-final. My father and I were terrified!

My brother Ben and I at our favourite restaurant, the Juboraj in Rhiwbina, celebrating the Grand Slam.

My grandfather Keith (to whom this book is dedicated) and my sister Holly at her wedding.

Captain for the first time, against the Barbarians and up against my hero Martyn Williams.

Giving Shane Williams a hand to bring down Keith Earls in the World Cup quarter-final against Ireland.

Huw Evans Images

My sports psychologist Andy McCann and I often refer to this photo as we like the level of focus in my face. Leading out Wales in the World Cup warm-up match against England in 2011.

Huw Evans Images

I have this on my wall at home – with fellow back-rowers Dan Lydiate and Toby Faletau after beating England in Cardiff in that warm-up match.

Courtesy of Sam Warburton

With WRU photographer Ben Evans, George North and Dan Lydiate after quad biking on the New Zealand coast.

In some space against Fiji
at the World Cup.

That tackle! I've got the ball!

Absolutely devastated on the
bench after being sent off.

Back in action after my ban, with Cardiff Blues against Racing Metro 92 in Paris.

I began to wear a headguard after the World Cup but it didn't last long!

Weight training in Auckland before the World Cup semi-final against France. I love the gym!

Leaving the cryotherapy chamber with Dan Lydiate who likes to mess around in there by singing or dancing!

Driving hard against Ireland in the Six Nations opener as Donncha O'Callaghan makes the tackle.

KRIOKOMORA · leczy · wzmacnia · odmładza

Soaring high against England at Twickenham, just winning the ball despite Geoff Parling's attentions.

The Triple Crown at Twickenham!

The captain's run on the eve of the Grand Slam match against France. Both my knee and thigh are heavily strapped.

Carrying hard in that France match.

The most surreal and incredible moment of my career. What I dreamed of since being a boy. The Grand Slam!

we made sure that we didn't do that in a second half that was as impressive as the first. Jamie scored again, but it was all down to George's break from halfway after an inside ball from Rhys. George exchanged passes with Rhys again near the line and could have scored himself, but, with his back to the line, instead popped the ball up to Jamie as he came charging through.

It was time for some changes as Toby, Rhys, Phillsy and Adam Jones all departed (to be replaced by Andy Powell, Stephen Jones, Lloyd Williams and Paul James), adding to the replacement of Bradley Davies by Alun Wyn Jones at half-time. Immediately Lloyd Burns showed great power to go over from a driving line-out, and then Leigh benefited when Fiji dropped a ball in attack and it was kicked downfield.

Kicked downfield by whom, though? Gethin Jenkins, of course, the supreme all-round footballer. Leigh won the foot race to score. Lloyd Williams added an eighth try, and then it was my chance . . .

My chance to desert the troops and leave them with fourteen men, that is. It wasn't my idea, it was Warren's. At the team run the day before the game, he had said to me: 'If we're doing well at the end of the game, I'm going to pull you off just to see how the players react.' I was a little bit shocked. 'Can you do that?' I asked. 'If I want to play with ten players, I can play with ten players,' he replied. And he was right. It was nothing more than a self-enforced sin-bin period. I wasn't allowed to tell any of the other players about it beforehand, although I think Ryan and Gethin knew.

Jamie had already gone off to be replaced by Jon Davies. So with just under ten minutes to go, Warren called me off. We had no replacements left. We were down to fourteen men. We were 59–0 up at the time, mind, but I still think it was a good idea. Warren is very shrewd like that. He is always thinking, always looking to come up with new ideas.

I'm not sure the players realised I was off until the next scrum. But they reacted really well and made the decisions Warren wanted them to. Dealing with yellow cards and being down to fourteen men is a difficult challenge defensively, especially at the set pieces. So this was good practice, and although I'd been a little bit wary at first, it was really good coaching.

And we did score another try through Jon Davies. Stephen Jones converted, his fourth conversion to add one more from Rhys, so that all nine tries had been converted.

The word 'ruthless' had been drummed into us all week ahead of the match, and we had delivered. We had also shown ambition – we spurned penalties to kick for touch numerous times in the second half – skill and commitment in defence. To ensure that Fiji did not score a single point was a target well achieved. Everyone put in a good shift on that front.

On the bus back from the game I had one of my weird feelings, just like the one I would have after being sent off against France. It was dark and I was sitting on my own, with my mind miles away, as the players often catch me doing. I just had this feeling that we were going to do something special. I caught myself smiling; I was that confident that we were going to be World Cup semi-finalists at the very least.

Out of the Pool of Death

There were some sore bodies the next morning at the usual pool recovery session. But there was also some fun. There was a particularly high diving board at the side of the pool, and we were all looking up at it and saying, 'No chance!'

Suddenly from nowhere Ryan Bevington appeared at the top of the board. Fair play to him. In he jumped, shouting 'Cannonball!', like the film *Anchorman* where Ron Burgundy jumps in.

That was it. Everybody went up and jumped or dived in, even though it was seriously scary. We were especially looking forward to Andy Powell's attempt. He was bound to do something really silly. Up to the board he went. To the edge of the board he ran. Then he stopped abruptly. He'd bottled it! We couldn't believe it. He went down to the floor of the board and began crawling backwards. You should have heard the abuse. Of all the people for it to happen to.

We were in good spirits. We were in the quarter-finals of the 2011 Rugby World Cup.

7

Ireland Quartered

It was the first time I had been away from my family for a birthday. Yes, there was some sadness in reaching twenty-three years of age on Wednesday 5 October 2011 without them being there, but it was three days away from a World Cup quarter-final against Ireland in Wellington. It was not a bad reason to be away from home.

I am a bit of a home boy, but only once on the trip had I really felt homesick before that day. I'd been on the phone to Rachel, and for some reason I'd found it really difficult to talk and had to hang up. She phoned back and I answered, but I just couldn't speak to her. I hung up again. It set her off in a real panic, but it was just that I was missing her and missing home so badly. I texted her to say just that.

Rugby players have emotions too; it is not all about a macho image. I sometimes talk to Rachel about how different I am on the field compared with off it. On the pitch I have to be aggressive, and have thrown myself into tackles that I probably shouldn't have. I do want, legally, to hurt someone if he gets on my nerves during a game. That's in the nature of the sport. There are certain characters you just want to put in their place, so I can be confrontational in that sense. Sometimes all it takes in a game is to receive a big hit, and it flicks a switch inside me. I can feel my blood boiling. There were times when I was a kid that my mum would shout, 'Stay calm, Sam!' She could see when I got riled up. Off the field, I'm completely different. I'm like my dad, who's a very calm, very relaxed and nonchalant sort of person. I've never been in a real fight in my life.

As I mentioned earlier, Rachel could not come out to New Zealand because she was taking her accountancy exams. At that point we had been living together for about eight months, and suddenly not seeing her every day was difficult to cope with at times. Of course, Skype is a wonderful modern invention, and on most days I would speak to Rachel, as well as my parents, and Ben and Holly. We were twelve hours ahead in New Zealand, so I would Skype at 8am every morning when everyone was at home after work at 8pm in Cardiff.

Rachel and I have been together since we were seventeen and at Whitchurch High School together. It's a real high-school sweetheart story, although I had to chase her for about two years before she would go out with me. We are both quite shy – I think that was the reason! Like her sister Sarah, Rachel played badminton for Wales. She played in European and World championships, and was hoping to make the Commonwealth Games in Delhi in 2010 to play doubles with her sister. Unfortunately that didn't work out, so she has concentrated on her accountancy. She does some coaching with local children and plays very occasionally. She's still very good. I played her once and she beat me 21–0 – not good for the self-esteem.

I had birthday cards from Rachel, my parents, and Ben and Holly, which I had not opened all trip. I'd looked after them like gold throughout the tour. Now at last it was time to open them. I just needed my room-mate Dan Lydiate to leave the room first as I wanted to do it in private. Eventually he did, and I opened all my cards. An emotional birthday had begun.

A long time earlier Huw Bennett had innocently slipped a question into conversation: 'If you could have any cake in the world, Warby, what would it be?' I immediately replied: 'A chocolate sponge, with chocolate icing and chocolate sauce.' A chocoholic? Never.

So later that day I was sitting down at the dinner table with all the other players when in walked Huw with a huge cake, just as I had inadvertently requested, as all the boys sang Happy Birthday. It was a nice moment. But it was followed by an awkward moment. Did I have some of the cake? Quite a few of the players had a sliver, but could I? It was only a few days before the quarter-final of the World Cup. In reality a sliver would not affect me. But the problem was that before every game I have to know in my own mind that I have done everything possible to prepare in terms of nutrition, sleep and both physical and mental training. The tiny percentages make a huge difference to me.

Chocolate is my treat after a game, but not before. Often after a game I go with Dan, and sometimes Ryan Bevington, to a local shop and buy three bars of chocolate. Cadbury's Fruit & Nut is my favourite by a long way. And then we go back to the room where Dan makes a cup of tea. He loves his tea. And I love looking forward to that moment after the game. After all the pressure and worry you can at last go back to your room, your body battered and bruised, throw your kit bag on the floor and lie back and relax. It is the one time when you are not thinking about the next game. The chocolate is the reward for all the hard work – the weekly treat.

There was to be no cake for me on my birthday then. I just couldn't do it. The coaches and rest of the management were happy because they ate most of it. I just had some fruit salad!

It was amazing how relaxed everyone was in the build-up to that Ireland game. At one team meeting we had some fun when Warren decided to show us a clip of the song 'Sam Our Captain', which had been created by a bloke born in Cardiff called Mark Berridge, who was then living in Australia. Sung to the tune of The Beach Boys' hit 'Sloop John B', it had become a bit of a favourite on the Internet and Ken Owens had alerted me to its presence. I think I already knew most of the lyrics before they were played to the team. Some of them are rather rude or disparaging of other players or referees, but the boys found it hilarious. We were all starting to get a lot more publicity now. Those quiet early weeks of the tournament were long gone.

I wouldn't say it worried me, but I mentioned to Andy McCann one day that things were hotting up, and he said: 'Why don't you come and do some relaxation stuff with me?' So that's what I did every night that week before the Ireland match, except the Friday night because I didn't want to be too lethargic on the day itself.

As I lay there listening to Andy's relaxation music for about thirty minutes, I would switch off completely from my rugby. We would talk a lot about music, and it was around this time that I started getting into Lenny Kravitz, the American singer known for playing the guitar, bass, drums, keyboards and percussion himself when recording.

But then I've always talked a lot about music. My dad loves his music. He has got about 600 metal albums. My uncle Andrew, who lives in Denmark, is also a real rock dude and is part of a band called Crime Club. So it's little wonder that I'm into my drumming. It is, after all, the heartbeat of heavy metal music.

When I was about seventeen I was in the Cardiff Blues Academy full time, but I was worried that I was doing nothing during the long afternoons after training. So I decided I had to start doing something, and it was either a PlayStation 3 or a drum kit. It was an easy choice really, especially as a mate of mine, Luke Robinson, or 'L-Rob' as we call him, was into his drums too. I was still living with my parents then so I told my dad what I was going to do. He could hardly complain about the noise because he had an electric guitar and amp.

He was soon showing me the basics, and I've just taken it from there. My first set of drums was quite cheap, just to see if I would get into it, so about a year later I bought a proper set, a Mapex kit with Sabian cymbals. It's the business.

Last year my uncle came over from Denmark and asked if I wanted to do a jamming session. I gave it a go and I loved it. He just said: 'Play any old beat and I'll come in with a riff.' And that's what we did. I felt like a right rock star.

I find it a great way to relax. Sometimes I even get my shirt off and get a real sweat up doing a good session. Luckily my house in Thornhill is detached, but I have got silencers for the kit so I don't think I've upset too many of the neighbours with the noise. The only problem is when Rachel gets home from work!

Andries Pretorius, who plays at Cardiff Blues with me, came round to my house a while ago, saw my drum kit, played a bit and now he's got himself an electric kit too. And Jamie Roberts plays the guitar and is always on about setting up a band. You might have to watch this space. We just have to find a singer. How about Leigh Halfpenny, the voice of an angel – he must be a contender . . .

Andy had relaxed me so much during that week of the Ireland game that I couldn't believe how much I enjoyed the team run the day before the match. Afterwards I even did some kicking.

There was a small possibility that, now we were into the knockout stages, the match could be decided by kicking at goal. The tournament rules stated that, if the scores were tied at the end of full time, first there would be extra time (two ten-minute periods), as happened in the 1995 and 2003 finals, which South Africa and England respectively won. If the scores were still level, teams would play a maximum of ten minutes of sudden death, with any score winning the contest (a bit like football's 'golden goal'). Then, as a last resort, there would be a kicking competition.

That was what had happened to Cardiff Blues when we lost the Heineken Cup semi-final against Leicester at the Millennium Stadium in 2009. And after all the backs had had a go, it was the back rowers who were sought out next. And poor Martyn Williams missed.

So Toby Faletau and I thought we'd take some kicks at goal, just in case. Dan had a go as well I think, but he was just terrible. There really was no point!

I've always fancied myself as a footballer. As I've mentioned, I'm from a footballing family, and football was definitely my first love. Nobody in my family had played rugby before. My maternal great-grandfather, George Reed, played football in the First Division for Leeds United, making 150 games in six seasons between the wars before injury cut short his career.

My brother Ben and I were the centre halves for our school team at Whitchurch, where we had a rather decent player on the left wing. Yes, from about the ages of eleven to sixteen we were in the same team as Gareth Bale, who has simply become one of the best footballers in the world. Our gameplan was always simple: clear the ball and get it to Gareth. Both Ben and I had trials with Cardiff City when we were fourteen, but it was then that I realised I wasn't going to make it and decided to concentrate on rugby.

Somebody in the Wales camp was clearly keen for me to rekindle my footballing skills, because before the South Africa game we had practised a new move, which involved me chipping over the oncoming defence. It was going to be from a shortened line-out and I was going to be the first receiver before surprising the South Africans by chipping over them. We practised it a lot in the build-up to that match, and I have to admit that it made me incredibly nervous. I stayed behind after training to practise it some more. I would stand behind the posts and try to just chip the ball over the crossbar, because that was the ideal height required. One day I must have done that fifty times before I was anywhere near satisfied.

But deep down I was happy that I was being asked to do it. People think of me as being all smash and bang, but I'd like to think that I've got a bit more finesse and skill than that, so this was an opportunity to show as much. After all, I'd done a couple of kick-and-chases against Italy in the 2011 Six Nations match. And most games I'd ever played at school I remember always doing at least one kick ahead during the game.

By the same token I was also dreading the moment Rhys Priestland might say on the field, 'Right, we're going to do the five-man chip,' or whatever it was called. Thankfully that call never did come, and we haven't practised it much since. You never know. Maybe one day.

One thing is for certain, though, if we ever do have a kicking competition to decide a match, Toby will definitely be kicking before I do. Neil Jenkins said as much when we were practising before the Ireland match. Toby and I decided to start by taking pot-shots from in front of the posts, and we both slotted our first kicks easily. By the time I was about to kick the second one, Jenks had wandered over to offer some advice. It was a bad move. I cracked immediately and missed the next three. I started thinking too much about my kicks. I never used to do that when I was young, in the nearby Caedelyn Park in Rhiwbina with Ben, when I was pretending to be a right-footed Jonny Wilkinson.

'Warbs, you're shocking,' said Jenks. 'If we have to go to the back row for a kicker it's you, Toby.'

And in fairness Toby is very good. He's such a natural athlete and sportsman that it's little surprise that he just stepped up and slotted his kicks.

One to watch out for is Bradley Davies. He's always dropping goals in training and I'm sure one day he's going to pull one out of the bag and do it in a game. He's always practising with Jenks. He calls him 'Neilo' and he'll shout, 'Don't move, Neilo,' and try to find him with a pinpoint kick.

There was one training session during the 2012 Six Nations, which I was sitting out through injury, that Warren decided to end with a game that was a version of Aussie Rules. You had to score with a drop-kick, and all of a sudden Bradley got the ball about 35 metres out and way on the right-hand side of the field. It was obvious that he had to find another member of his team nearer the posts before they could consider scoring. Well, it was obvious to everyone apart from Bradley, who attempted an outrageous long-range drop-goal.

It only went over! You should have seen the scenes. Bradley was running around the field in celebration, as though he'd just scored the winner in an FA Cup Final. 'You've got to pick me after that, Warren,' he was shouting. 'You've got to pick me!' It was hilarious.

I hope Dan Lydiate is reading this. I'm about to tell him something he doesn't know.

Dan is very laid back, but when it's time for the game he is also hugely focused and aggressive. He knows that, of course, but what he doesn't know is that, being his room-mate all this time, I can tell exactly when the switch is flicked and he is mentally ready for the game. It can happen at various times on the day before a game. We will be sitting in the room having a cup of tea, and he will suddenly turn very serious and slip into the conversation something like 'We've got to ******* smash 'em tomorrow!' That's it. Dan's ready.

What Dan also doesn't know is that I always tell Rhys Long, the team analyst, when Dan is ready. Rhys will see me during the day before the game and ask: 'Has he said it yet?'

'No, not yet.'

Maybe a couple of hours later I might see Rhys again. 'Has he said it yet?' he will ask again.

'Yep, he's said it now. He's ready!'

And Dan was certainly ready for the Ireland game. We both were. Just as we were both a little bit miffed about all the coverage the Irish back row was getting ahead of that game. Every newspaper that was left on the breakfast table seemed to have something in it about Sean O'Brien, Jamie Heaslip and

Stephen Ferris, and about how they were going to win the back-row battle. It wasn't their fault, of course. Those three are top blokes and superb players. They don't write the articles.

But it was really annoying me and Dan. We are very similar in that we both want to be the very best. We share the same values, which is why we get on so well.

We spoke to Toby about all this coverage for the Irish back row, but he is so chilled out and nonchalant that he just said 'Whatever,' and got on with his own quiet way of doing things. Toby really is an amazing character. I spoke to Andy McCann about him, and how a sports psychologist might deal with him. Andy said that a character like him you just leave alone and let him do his own thing. It obviously works for him, and he does not seem to have any worries or concerns about his play.

It was great news that Dan was fit for this quarter-final after his ankle injury. He was one of four changes from the side that had beaten Fiji 66–0. Shane Williams returned on the wing, with Leigh Halfpenny moving to full back. Jon Davies replaced Scott Williams at centre, Dan replaced Ryan Jones, and Alun Wyn Jones was to start instead of Bradley. It was the first time in the tournament that Warren had thirty fit players from which to choose, and I know that he deliberated long and hard about the selection, but there was no doubt that those picked had been in excellent form throughout.

We were confident, even if nobody else was. We seemed to be routinely written off. Yes, Ireland had stunned Australia in the group stages, but we'd beaten Ireland the last time we'd played them: 19–13 in the Six Nations in Cardiff. That it had come from a controversial Mike Phillips try did not matter. We had won.

I was confident too, even if I was sick on the morning of the game. That was more of an accident than any horrendous pre-match nerves. I generally have quite a weak stomach and struggle to eat anything solid before a game. I usually have a specially made carbohydrate drink called Vitargo, maybe some pancakes, some rice pudding and a banana, while others will wolf down a full-blown chicken pasta meal. I just couldn't do that.

I was in our hotel in Oriental Bay, Wellington, having a shower when I suddenly started coughing. It was a bad move. If I have a cold and just blow my nose I can start gagging and then be sick. Sadly, that's what happened here on the day of the World Cup quarter-final. I was sick all over the shower wall! My big worry was that I wouldn't have any energy inside me, and I was going to need plenty; I was playing in a World Cup quarter-final in a few hours. I quickly dried myself, got dressed and ran back downstairs to get some more food inside me. And I now make sure that I don't cough before a game!

If my day hadn't started how I might have wanted, the game itself could not have started any better. We scored after just two minutes. The ball was claimed by Jamie Roberts from a high kick, then first I went quite close to the line, before the ball was recycled and transferred right for Toby to make a huge charge that nearly brought him a try. But when it was recycled again Mike Phillips fed Leigh Halfpenny, who put Shane

Williams in at the corner. Rhys Priestland converted brilliantly from the touchline and we were 7–0 up. It was the perfect start, just what we wanted. It's obviously a lot easier to stay ahead of the game than to chase it.

We knew Ireland would come at us strongly then, and they did. O'Brien went close after a driving line-out, but we were saved by some great defence from Mike Phillips and Dan. Twice Ireland had spurned penalties and kicked for the corner, and twice we had repelled them.

Then Rob Kearney went through the middle and we were penalised so that Ronan O'Gara made it 7–3. Leigh Halfpenny kicked a monster penalty from near halfway to make it 10–3 after half an hour, and that's the way it stayed until half-time. We lost Luke Charteris during that interval to a shoulder injury, but the fact that he had already made a remarkable sixteen tackles in that time shows what a massive defensive effort we were making.

Just after the break Ireland scored. It was one of those instances where the ball looks as if it has gone loose and the attack has been stopped, but Conor Murray's pass was picked up by Ferris who found Tommy Bowe running around him. Even then Bowe's pass bounced before it found Keith Earls, but Earls slid from a long way out to avoid Phillsy's tackle and score. O'Gara converted from the touchline, and it was 10–10 after forty-five minutes.

We needed something brilliant. And Phillsy duly provided it. Alun Wyn Jones had driven powerfully through the centre of a ruck to make some good ground, but the ball had been slow in appearing from the subsequent ruck. Phillsy waited and waited. Then suddenly he picked up and darted left. There wasn't much room, but he handed off Gordon D'Arcy and then dived for the corner. Bowe was covering across, but Phillsy somehow managed to dot the ball down while in mid-air. It was an amazing finish.

Just over ten minutes later we saw more brilliance. This time it came from Jon Davies. We were going right, and when Jon took the ball from Rhys Priestland it did not appear that too much was on. But Jon is exceptionally quick and strong. He went between Cian Healy and Earls, and shrugged off Bowe and replacement scrum-half Eoin Reddan for our third try. Rhys converted and it was 22–10 with fourteen minutes to go. That was it. We made sure Ireland didn't score again. We didn't score either, although Rhys, rather unluckily, hit a post for a second time in the match with a penalty. It had been a magnificent big-match performance and it was left to Huw Bennett to boot the ball off the field and the final whistle to go.

Phillsy was made man of the match, not just for his eye-catching try but for his general control of play. But there were so many heroes yet again. Rhys was superb at fly-half, Jamie had a monstrous game and Dan was outstanding. The scrummage was excellent, with Adam Jones really on top of his game. And the line-out was good too – Gethin Jenkins even won three of them, two from Irish throws! I was also pretty happy with my eighteen tackles.

Huge credit should go to Warren and the coaching staff.

Firstly the selection was spot on. There were close calls involving Leigh, Jon and Rhys, and they all delivered in a big way. Then there were the tactics. The coaches were quite brilliant in that regard.

When Ireland had beaten Wales 17–15 in 2009 to win the Grand Slam in Cardiff, they had used high cross-kicks to good effect. They were clearly hoping to do something similar in this game in a wet and windy Wellington, and wanted the taller Bowe to out-jump Shane Williams. And with Bowe picked on the right wing and Shane on the left, it looked as if that might happen.

But Warren had no intention of playing Shane on the left wing, even if he was going to wear the No. 11 shirt. For most of the game George North played on the left and Shane on the right. Ireland tried a cross kick early to Bowe, but George was there to mark it.

The other pre-determined tactic was that we were going to tackle low. Ireland have a lot of powerful ball-carriers and it was decided that we had to stop them going anywhere, to scythe them down immediately. It is something we practise a lot. Shaun Edwards will say at the end of a training session: 'Right, it's time for some low tackle extras.' And we will do a drill whereby the player to be tackled holds a tackle shield against his shins so that he does not get injured. Then he runs sideways and the tackler will come flying in low and try to get his arms around the man and lock them in. It is where Dan is in his element. He is simply the best at doing it. Paul James is pretty good at it too.

There used to be a lot of ego attached to the reading of tackle statistics after a game. Everyone was looking for their 'tackle pluses', which are tackles in which you knock your man back behind the gain line. There is the 'tackle zero' in which you hit your man on the gain line and you both go down there with no ground made either way. And then there is the 'tackle minus' whereby you are taken a distance backwards in making the tackle. This was a game where you had to leave your ego in the dressing room. There were a lot of 'tackle zeroes' and 'tackle minuses' in this game: it was not about trying to smash them backwards, it was about chopping them down immediately. Warren told us afterwards that O'Brien had twenty-one carries in the match, and only made 21 metres. And I subsequently heard that their whole back row made forty-four carries and only made 44 metres. That was a great effort from us. We stopped them at source.

We also combated their 'choke tackle' well. During the week, we'd talked a lot about that tactic, so encouraged by their defensive coach Les Kiss. It had been particularly effective for Ireland when they had beaten Australia. The theory of it is that if the ball is held up in a maul, then the attacking side lose the ball. Ireland's first tackler tries to hold the attacker up, and then a colleague comes in to 'choke' the ball. All the time the Irish players will be shouting 'Maul, maul, maul,' to the referee.

I was asked my opinion on it in a team meeting, and I was very blunt in my assessment. One of those players performing the 'choke tackle' has his back to us, the attacking side. To me he is no different from a player lying on the wrong side of a ruck. He is trying to kill your ball. Old-style rucking may not be permitted these days, but there are still ways and means of getting a player on the wrong side of a ruck out of the way. So it should be the same with a player with his back to you in a 'choke tackle'. You can do it legally. You can hurt an opponent legally. You can still go in there and smash him!

And that's what we did. Along with the low tackling, we had got the better of them at the contact area. Against South Africa and Samoa we had said that we had to be nastier than them in the physical stakes, but this was taking it to another level. We really did have to be considerably more physical than Ireland.

The outcome was a famous victory. We were in a World Cup semi-final now. What an achievement. I'd always thought that possible, as I've said before, but the realisation was still awesome. We deserved this. All that work we'd done in Poland and thereafter was worth it.

One of my favourite moments of the whole World Cup is captured in a picture that was taken of me and George just after the final whistle had gone. We are hugging each other and we are just so happy. There is also another picture of me shaking hands with Warren, both of us with huge smiles on our faces.

There were more Irish fans in the stadium than Welsh – the bus journey to the ground had been through a sea of green – but our fans were still quite magnificent. Afterwards we walked around the stadium to thank them and we all sang 'Delilah'. Before that, whenever I heard that song, I thought of warming up in the Millennium Stadium when it is sung before the game. But now whenever I hear it, I think of that quarter-final win over Ireland in Wellington. It is a wonderful memory.

Had we lost that game, we would have been on a plane home the very next day. I suppose some of us might even have packed a few things just in case. But now we were staying, and everybody was absolutely buzzing. It was the sort of occasion on which anybody would want to celebrate. But we knew we couldn't. It was only a week until an even bigger game. 'I'm on water,' I told the press afterwards. 'Maybe some of the boys will have one or two [beers], but they have to realise we've got the biggest game of our lives next week. We haven't won anything yet, we've got to keep our feet on the ground.'

Telling players that they cannot go out and drink is never easy, especially when they are so excited after such a massive achievement. There are some players who like a drink and I have got no problem with that. So, as someone who rarely drinks, when judging such things I know that I have to be careful. I would never make a decision on my own in this regard. I always consult Warren and Ryan Jones, as well as some other senior players. You've got to do what's good for team morale.

If you've beaten, say, Namibia, you don't feel the need to say anything after the game about drinking. With all due respect to Namibia, there shouldn't be any real need to celebrate excessively. But after this huge win I did feel that something needed to be said. It was not like our trips to Poland where there had been a 'dry board'. There was no 'dry board' at the World Cup.

Some players had a drink now and again. Some went out and had a good time. I remember one night when Mike Phillips and Jon Davies came up to me and asked if they could go out. They said they didn't want to drink much, they just wanted to get out and about. Some players need that, and I respect that. They said they would be back by midnight, and they were. I trusted them. Not once during the World Cup did any of the players let each other down.

Sometimes members of the management, like Adam Beard and Dan Baugh (a good man to have on speed-dial if you ever get into any trouble), would go out with the players, just to make sure that nothing untoward happened and that they were back to the hotel by the time specified.

So that night after beating Ireland I just said that nobody should go 'mental', that they could go out to a local bar if they wanted, but that everyone had to be back at the hotel by 12.30am. And there were to be no shots or shorts!

Everyone was fine. It had been a great day. And a great night.

If we thought the attention on us had been ramped up before that match, it was nothing compared to afterwards. We were in for a shock. It just went mad. When my parents arrived they said it was 'bonkers' back home, and that's how it felt.

I only had to look at my Twitter feed to know that. Twitter had been a topic of debate amongst the squad before we left for New Zealand. When we were at Heathrow, Warren and Alan Phillips had asked me to get a decision from the players as to whether Twitter should be allowed during the trip. I got the impression that neither of them was that keen on it being used.

During the summer we had had a talk on the dangers of social networking, and as a result I had closed down my Facebook account. I was just getting too many requests to do things on there, whether it was for tickets or appearances at club dinners. I know people will say that they are only asking once, but when you are getting fifty or more people asking the same thing, it can be really difficult. As I've said before, I try as hard as I can to help people out, but the truth is that you can't help everybody. As the person giving the talk quite rightly pointed out, using an example of a player who I won't name: 'You've got 1500 friends on Facebook and it is simply not possible for anyone to have that many close friends who should be seeing the stuff you put on Facebook.'

I was sceptical of Twitter at first too. But I had a good chat with Ryan Jones about it and he said that, if used correctly, it can be a really good tool for your profile and that of the team. I think Warren and Thumper thought that I was being bullied a bit by the senior players about this, but I wasn't. I wanted to see what the reaction was. So we decided that we would give Twitter a go for a week and then reassess. It was stressed that there should be nothing mentioned in terms of selection or stuff that happened at training or in the team room, but it was felt it was a good way to interact with the fans.

So Tavis Knoyle, used as our announcer on the bus a lot because he is so funny, was told to tell the squad just that. There was going to be a week's trial with Twitter, and Paul James and Huw Bennett were to monitor its use.

Not that I was actually on Twitter myself then. Only about a third of the squad were. And not that I had any real intention of being so. But during the first week in Wellington I was sharing with Lloyd Williams, and we seemed to spend most of our spare time playing golf on our iPads using the Tiger Woods PGA Tour 12 game. In fact most of the boys seemed to be doing that during the first week.

I thought: 'I've got to do something else other than this.' Scott Williams was in the room with me and Lloyd, and they were trying very hard to get me to go on Twitter. 'Just get on there and see how many followers you can get,' they said. At the time Jamie Roberts had about 15,000 followers and all the boys considered him an A-list celebrity. I think Lloyd was on about 1,000.

So I just went on for a laugh, to see how many followers I could get in a day. All the boys tweeted that I was on and within a day I had about 1,500 to 2,000 followers. Lloyd and Scott were gutted!

As I write, the 'Doc' is still miles ahead of the rest of us, and he is always bragging about it! I'm chasing him, though. As I write he has 79,350 followers; I have 70,427.

After a week we reviewed it, and there had been no problems. Even Warren said, 'I have been incredibly impressed by the maturity of this group of players. They are making a call themselves in terms of Twitter. Apparently there is a Twitter account of myself out there, but I can assure you it is a fake one. We're just making sure that we are professional and responsible.'

All the players have eventually joined, apart from Justin Tipuric. I started a campaign to get him on during the Six Nations in 2012, but he's just not interested. I did get Dan Lydiate on there during the World Cup, however. I tweeted: 'Who wants Dan Lydiate to join Twitter?' And I had so many responses that I showed them to him. He was impressed. So he went on, and before he knew it, he had 5,000 followers.

But it was after the Ireland match that Twitter went really mad. It was then that the hash tag #samwarburtonfacts started trending. Before the match it had been Irish fans who were posting a series of #seanobrienfacts about Sean O'Brien. Now the Welsh fans were taking their turn and posting fictional facts about me, just like those written about the cult action star Chuck Norris and the fictional hero Jack Bauer from *24*.

Some days I would spend half an hour reading all the new ones. They would be along the lines of: 'Sam Warburton doesn't need life insurance; life needs Sam Warburton insurance #samwarburtonfacts'. Or: 'Before Voldemort goes to sleep he checks under the bed for Sam Warburton #samwarburtonfacts'. But my favourite and probably the best known was the one related to my rugby exploits in New Zealand: 'The AA have gone out of business. Sam Warburton beat them to every breakdown. #samwarburtonfacts'.

*

Ireland Quartered

Ever since I was a kid I had always wanted to be a major sports-person. Now I was leading my country in the World Cup and all this was happening to me. It was surreal. But probably not as surreal as what happened next at the World Cup.

I've dealt with that already, and it's certainly not my intention to deal with it again. I found it difficult enough the first time.

8

Halloween Horrors

It was not the ideal time to return home from New Zealand. After seeing the World Cup final and attending the IRB awards dinner, I got back to Cardiff just before Halloween. And there is no better excuse to knock on your door than Halloween.

It seemed that a few more people knew where I lived in Thornhill than was the case when I left for the World Cup. One evening just after I'd got back, Derwyn was at my house because we had plenty to talk about. We had to plot a way through all the inevitable media stuff resulting from the World Cup. And there on my doorstep was instant evidence of how difficult it was going to be to keep a low profile over the following months.

The doorbell didn't stop ringing. Rachel was trying to revise for her exams upstairs, and I was downstairs trying to talk seriously with Derwyn. It wasn't just kids coming to the door doing their 'trick or treat', either. There were parents waiting at the bottom of the drive with their cameras too.

In the end Derwyn had had enough and started answering the door himself. I think the kids were a bit alarmed to see a 6ft 10in bald bloke standing there growling at them!

I might have been able to avoid the kids that night, but I had to face the press sometime. I had to tell them what I thought about my red card. So the week after I arrived home, on Thursday 3 November, Cardiff Blues organised a press conference and photo shoot for all their returning World Cup players. So alongside me dressed in the new pink change kit were Bradley Davies, Gethin Jenkins, Lloyd Williams, Jamie Roberts and Leigh Halfpenny. The event started at 12.45pm, and I didn't leave much before 6pm. The others had gone long before.

It was savage. There is no other word for it. I knew I had to do it and I'd like to think I was civil and polite throughout, while giving everyone – photographers, journalists and broadcasters – everything they wanted. But five hours' worth? Wow.

As I mentioned earlier, I hadn't been told what to say. There was no pre-conceived plan that I was going to admit that I agreed with Alain Rolland's decision. But that was what I did. As I have already said, I still think it was rather unfair, but by the letter of the law Rolland was right. So the next day the headlines screamed out: 'Warburton: Rolland was right to show me World Cup red card.'

This is the gist of what I said: 'I have seen it played back, the tackle is a lot uglier than I thought it was at the time. When I looked at it on the replays it looked worse than I thought it was. I didn't intend to do anything like that and I had only had a yellow card in my career up until that point so it was a shock to get a red, but there was nothing I could do and I just had to support the boys for the rest of that match and the remaining game against Australia. The IRB said if you lift up a player and drop him it's a red card, and that's exactly what I did. I can't complain. There was no point in appealing against it. I didn't have a leg to stand on.'

Derwyn had organised for me and Rachel to stay at Claridge's in Mayfair for a few days the previous weekend. It would be OK down there in London. Nobody would recognise me. I could relax.

Very kindly one of the porters took our bags up to the room for us. We thanked him and gave him a tip. 'Thank you, sir,' he said to me. 'By the way, it was never a red card.'

You couldn't make it up. Rachel and I just laughed at each other.

After that mammoth press day I needed another break, so that weekend we went to stay in the Bath Spa Hotel, as due to my three-week ban I wasn't available until 7 November. So I wasn't playing in the local derby against Newport Gwent Dragons on the Friday night, a match that was eventually called off because of a waterlogged pitch.

Talk of the red card wasn't going to go away easily. Don't get me wrong, there was an awful lot of support too. I had loads of letters, emails, phone calls and texts from people saying, 'Keep your head up.' I really appreciated all those messages of support. I even had a few hugs from women I didn't know, but who obviously felt sorry for me! I'd be in the motorway services and somebody would walk past and say, 'It wasn't a red card.' Or I'd be in my local Sainsbury's and people would come up to me and want to chat about the incident. I could understand that they wanted to talk to me about it, but what they didn't understand was that I'd already spoken about it a thousand times.

My brother had given me some advice on that. He had said never forget when you are talking to people about the World Cup, it might be the fiftieth time you've spoken about it, but it might be their first. He said I had to be patient, and he was right.

There was the odd prank at the Blues, but that was to be expected. On pretty much my first day back training with them, they gave me a red bib to wear when everyone else was wearing green. Martyn Williams had warned me that sort of thing might happen. It happened to him after he missed that kick in the kicking competition against Leicester in the Heineken Cup semi-final in 2009. To be honest, I thought I would get a lot more stick than I did. But it was still quite raw.

I didn't realise how raw it was until the week before we played the one-off Test against Australia at the Millennium Stadium on 3 December. I went round to my mum and dad's house with Rachel. Ben was there, as was my sister Holly, with her husband Chris Haime. There had been a programme made called *That Semi-Final* and Ben had been interviewed for it. My dad asked me if I wanted to see it. My mum said I probably shouldn't because I might get upset.

I hadn't seen any footage of the game, apart from looking at my tackle on YouTube. But I said that I would just watch Ben's interview. I saw him there in his Newport Gwent Dragons kit (where he is a physio) and I was so proud of him. I said, 'Come on, let's watch the whole thing.'

Again, my mum was concerned. 'Are you sure?' she asked.

'Let's see it,' I said. 'I wouldn't mind seeing what it was like from other people's perspectives.'

So there I sat in the lounge, with Rachel and my family, and we watched the programme. I hadn't realised how much Wales had stopped for the World Cup. They showed a clip of the 62,000 fans watching the semi-final on big screens in the Millennium Stadium at 9am. They were all going ballistic. They were so passionate.

Then I got my red card. And it showed the whole stadium in silence. It was like a morgue. You could see the devastation on people's faces. It really got to me. I thought: 'I can't do this in front of my family.'

But I did. My emotions got the better of me. It sounds a bit cringeworthy, but it suddenly hit home how many people it had affected. All those feelings I had experienced in the dressing room in Auckland came flooding back. I realised how many people I could have upset. I was devastated.

Thankfully I can make more of a joke of it now. As I was writing this book I was involved in some filming for MTV's

Made, where a young lad from Kingston in London was given specialist coaching and advice in his quest to become a professional rugby player. It concluded with a game at Esher RFC between the Esher Fireflies team and Kingston University. I was watching and was all miked up to make comments, when, inevitably I suppose, somebody made a tip tackle. Just as inevitably the player wasn't sent off, so all eyes turned to me. 'Hey, I got sent off for that!' I shouted jokingly at the referee.

If my mind was still a little sensitive when I returned home from New Zealand, that was nothing compared to my body. To be totally honest, it was in bits. The knee that had started troubling me after the win over Samoa in Hamilton was still causing me a lot of grief. So as soon as I got home I had a synovial fluid injection to lubricate it. But it was still causing me pain so I also had a cortisone injection in it. Then when that didn't settle it completely, I had another cortisone in the other side of the knee.

Meanwhile I was also having problems with my right shoulder. It felt like it was hanging off, so I had a cortisone injection in that too. Did I feel like a pin cushion? Yep!

I felt that I had to have these injections because I didn't feel that I could come back to the Blues and not play. We all knew that the World Cup had created a huge interest in Welsh rugby and that fans wanted to see us all on our return.

This is an issue that I have already spoken about on the record. Something needs to be done in terms of the number of games our international players are expected to play. Maybe dual contracts between the WRU and one's region are the way to go. Every player has a duty to perform for his region as well his country, but I find that if I play more than twenty games a year I just get injured. That is the way the game is going at the moment, because it is so physical. An international game, I would say, could be the equivalent of two regional games, with no disrespect. With regional rugby, there are certain fixtures in the RaboDirect Pro12 that are not as intense. If the regions and the union could work on that twenty-games-a-year guideline to get the best out of players, similar to Ireland, that would be great.

I know from talking to players who come back from international duty that they want to play for their region. That's where they are paid, but your body, after you have taken a battering in international rugby, just won't let you do that. It's hard because you want to fulfil your duty with the region, but you also don't want to play at 60–70 per cent. It is about getting the balance right.

And that was my problem now. I was expected to come back and perform for the Blues in the Heineken Cup, but in reality my body was creaking. Before the Six Nations began in early 2012, I did manage to play in eight games (six Heineken Cup matches and two RaboDirect Pro12 fixtures), as well as the Test against Australia in December. I tried to get on with it as best I could, but I don't think I delivered my best performances because my body simply wasn't up to it. In fact I was only happy with my performances in four out of those eight matches for the Blues.

I think a lot of the other World Cup players were the same.

The only one who didn't seem to be too affected was Toby Faletau, but then he is indestructible. Or at least we thought he was until he broke a bone in his hand during the first Test in Australia in the summer of 2012. Until then he just turned up to training every day, did his work brilliantly and went home. Some of the performances he was putting in for the Newport Gwent Dragons after the World Cup astounded the rest of us. We were just looking at him and thinking: 'How on earth is he doing that?'

Fate naturally decreed that my first game back for the Blues was against a French side. I had only played against two French sides before – Castres and Toulouse – but now I found myself up against Racing Metro 92 out in Paris at the Stade Yves Du Manoir. It was going to be interesting to see how the locals reacted to me.

Should I have played? Well, the day before the game we were doing the team run, and Jamie Roberts came up to me and said bluntly, 'Warbs, you're not fit to play, mate.' He could see that I was limping, as there was still quite a bit of fluid on my knee and it was making it feel unstable. 'Go and see the physio and tell him you can't play.'

But I couldn't. I didn't want to let the Blues down. I would have felt too guilty. So for the remainder of that day and most of the night before that match, I iced my knee using the special 'Game Ready' ice-machine. It is a brilliant machine that you just fill with ice and water, attach the wrap to the injured part of your body, select the pressure and time settings you want, and then let the machine circulate cold water and pneumatically apply compression to your injury.

Sadly because I've had so many injuries in the last year, I've had to use it a lot, but it is very effective – certainly effective enough to allow me to play.

As it was, Jamie left the field injured as early as the eleventh minute in this match, which was a blow, especially as our second row James Down had suffered a horrific fracture dislocation of his ankle after just two minutes. So for us to win 26–20 away from home, with tries from Tau Filise and Alex Cuthbert and 16 points from Dan Parks' boot, was some achievement.

And surprisingly there was little reaction from the French crowd or opposition. I had a quick exchange of smirks with the France second row Lionel Nallet when he ran on as a replacement, but that was it.

I hadn't done a great deal in the game. Then late on I saw my chance to make a mark. Racing Metro were moving the ball from left to right and I was positioned in the middle of the field in our defensive line. Replacement fly-half Jon Wisniewski threw a flat pass to another replacement, prop Eddy Ben Arous. It was perfect for a big hit, and I lined him up and smashed him. This time, though, I held on to him as I hit him backwards. It felt good. I was back. I'd made my first big hit since the semi-final incident. Apparently this became an Internet hit too.

Not that tip tackles were going to go away. The previous weekend the Scarlets Stephen Jones had been yellow carded for one on the Ospreys' Tommy Bowe in the local derby at the Liberty Stadium. It was quite naturally compared to my tackle.

And in our next Heineken Cup match, a week later at home

to London Irish, I was right on the spot when Irish's Steve Shingler, who was then trying to qualify for Scotland even though his brother Aaron was to make his international debut for Wales in the 2012 Six Nations, made a horrible-looking spear tackle on our centre Dafydd Hewitt. He was instantly given a red card, and I thought the referee Jerome Garces had no choice in that instance. It was a bad tackle. I knew the camera was going to pan on to me again, so I made sure I said nothing.

No one else said anything either, and we got on with winning the game 24–18, even though it was hardly a vintage performance. We were 10–0 up when the Irish went down to fourteen men, but we could not take advantage and they fought back hard. Lloyd Williams was outstanding for us, scoring a superb try just before half-time. Hooker Rhys Thomas also scored and Parks did the rest with his kicking.

We were unbeaten in Europe after two rounds, and so were the other three Welsh regions. Things were certainly looking up in Welsh rugby.

But just as I was getting used to be being back with the Blues, it was time to head off into the Wales camp again for the Australia Test. I'd only just about remembered all the Blues calls. Now I had to remember the Wales ones again. It can be a pain getting the jargon and terminology right when it comes to moves. Blues calls have been known to be called for Wales and vice versa, but I'm not naming any names!

The other thing is that the patterns of play are quite different between Wales and the Blues. At the Blues we like to go wide quite quickly, and with Wales it's very much a case of earning the right to go wide by taking it on up front. They are two different game plans.

It was strange playing a one-off Test, as there are usually a series of autumn internationals. And we were missing some key players. Adam Jones, Alun Wyn Jones, Luke Charteris, Jon Davies and Paul James were all injured, while the players based in France, like Mike Phillips, James Hook and Andy Powell, were unavailable.

But it did give an opportunity to some others. The Blues prop Scott Andrews made his first Test start, as did the Blues' Lloyd Williams at scrum-half. And this was the first time we had winger Alex Cuthbert in the squad. He was on the bench, but he was already exciting everyone. He'd been playing really well for the Blues and deserved his call-up. I remember watching him on the sevens circuit about a year before. I couldn't get over his pace. When I'd joined up with the Blues again I'd seen this at first hand. He was running round almost everyone. He looked as natural a finisher as Leigh Halfpenny. He's a good 6ft 5in and almost 16st – he's just like George North, except his legs aren't quite as big. But then whose legs are as big as George's?

Alex was on the bench because this was Shane Williams's last Test. It was great that Shane was getting the opportunity to finish on home soil. As soon as we'd gathered in camp, it was made very clear to us all that this game was all about Shane. And rightly so. It was his 87th Test (he'd also played four for the British and Irish Lions), and he is quite simply a Wales legend. Whatever Shane wanted, we did.

The Tuesday before the Test was called Shane's Day. We all wore Shane masks. There were pictures plastered all over the team room of him from when he started at Amman United and Neath, right the way through to his Wales and British Lions days. It was the consensus amongst us that there were some shocking haircuts along the way!

His family were asked to come and eat us with us at meal times, which I thought was a really nice touch. And Warren Gatland made him coach for the day. Not that he'd told him that beforehand, I don't think. But Shane is a sharp and funny guy. He was immediately off doing impressions of Warren and the other coaches. He had us in stitches. But he actually ran the sessions really well.

This was one of many reasons why this match was very emotional. Shane led us out to a massive standing ovation and he wore a special shirt with the word 'Diolch' – Welsh for thank you – on the chest. Then there was a minute's silence, which broke into spontaneous applause, in memory of the late Wales football manager Gary Speed, who had died the previous Sunday.

It was also emotional for me because it was the first time I had played for Wales since the red card, and the first time playing at the Millennium Stadium since 62,000 had been there watching that World Cup semi-final. My bottom lip was going a little bit during the anthems, but I managed to hold it together.

I should mention that I was happy being captain, after all the fuss I'd made earlier. I was now totally at ease doing the job, but that is not to say that I took it for granted that I would be doing it. Matthew Rees was back in the squad, after all, although he was only on the bench. I didn't have a clue what was going through Warren's mind, but this time when he asked me I did not dither. I felt like a captain now.

We lost the match 24–18, but Shane engineered a fairytale finish as he scored in stoppage time, screaming loudly as he crossed the line and then doing a somersault as he scored. The noise was unbelievable, just like when he had scored at the death in the 2010 Six Nations win over Scotland. I'd come on as a replacement in that match, and it was just so loud that you couldn't hear the player next to you, even if he was shouting. This was the same: a fitting end to the career of a great.

I had been really looking forward to this game. First there was a chance to play against David Pocock. Before that semi-final I had been thinking that, whatever happened, I would get to play against either Pocock or Richie McCaw, as Australia and New Zealand were contesting the other semi-final. I was going to be playing in either a World Cup final or a third-place play-off. I hadn't given a millisecond's thought to the possibility of being sent off and then being banned for the next match.

It was not the first time I had faced Pocock – I had met him in age-group rugby, as well as in a full international in Cardiff in 2010 – but it didn't make the contest any easier, even if he did not return after half-time because of an ankle injury.

I reckon he's the toughest one to play against. His strength over the ball and his timing are impeccable. There are a lot of strong, squat people in the 'jackal', but he's the best at it because of his timing. He's also the toughest to shift off the ball.

It was also another opportunity to take a southern hemisphere scalp. Wales had beaten Australia in 2008, but had only won twice in their previous eighteen matches against them. This was the next step. We'd done superbly at the World Cup, but we hadn't beaten a southern hemisphere side. I kept saying to the press and to the players, 'There's no point putting in good performances in the northern hemisphere and then just coming close against the southern sides.'

Sadly, that's what happened again. We were 6–3 up at half-time through two Rhys Priestland penalties, but then on forty-nine minutes Leigh Halfpenny was sin-binned for tackling James O'Connor without the ball as O'Connor chased Berrick Barnes' kick ahead.

While Leigh was off we conceded twenty-one points, three tries for Will Genia, Lachie Turner and Barnes, all converted by O'Connor. That was seriously disappointing. It wasn't Leigh's fault, though. He had saved a try. He'd saved us seven points, we had given away twenty-one. We should never have conceded as many as we did in that period. As I've mentioned before, we practise a lot with fourteen men for such situations. This was what Warren was thinking about when he took me off before the end of the Fiji World Cup match.

But we just didn't react properly. Then our heads went down and the Australians were really clinical in taking their chances. At 24–6 down it was a long road back. We did score through Rhys Priestland with thirteen minutes to go, and again, of course, through Shane and his 58th Test try for Wales. But we had lost to a southern hemisphere side yet again.

There was barely time to reflect on it, though, because six days later I was back playing for the Blues at home against Edinburgh in the Heineken Cup. We won 25–8, and I felt that I had a good game. Good enough in fact to be named man of the match.

There was a poor crowd in attendance at the Cardiff City Stadium – just over 6,000 for a big European game – giving rise to the concerns that eventually led to the Blues deciding to return to the Arms Park for the 2012/13 season. That is a decision I wholeheartedly agree with. It was always difficult to say as much while we were at the Cardiff City Stadium, because there were obviously reasons for going there and it would have been wrong to upset the apple cart. But if you ask any of the players, they will say the same: the Arms Park is better. It has so much history. It was where I wanted to play when I was growing up, and it is where I want to play now.

On the Tuesday after that Edinburgh match I received some tragic news. My grandfather Keith Kennedy had died in the University Hospital, Heath, in Cardiff. He had not been well for a long time, and had fought cancer bravely. But it was still a terrible shock.

My grandmother had passed away when I was four, so this was the first family member I could remember losing. And it hit me hard. I had been close to my granddad. He was a Rhiwbina boy too, and he would come round to our house every Friday. He would often say the same thing to me and Ben: 'Life is simple: you get out of it what you put into it.' It is so true, and I have certainly stuck by that motto. When I am struggling at training, or if I ever lack a little bit of motivation to go training, I think of my granddad and what he used to say. That gets me going.

We had Blues training on the morning that I found out about my granddad. I was all over the place, and didn't really know how to react. I didn't want to tell anyone because I didn't want sympathy, but the trouble was that I was late for training, and I got a lot of stick about that. I got some playful banter from the players, but the coaches really slated me.

We were playing Edinburgh again the following Friday. It was a huge game. We had won those first three games in our pool but we hadn't got any bonus points. We needed to win again badly.

People react in different ways to bereavement. Bradley Davies's mum had passed away in 2010 and he had played a week later against France, and had played brilliantly. But I was not coping in the same way.

I just couldn't get motivated for the match. With the benefit of hindsight I should not have played. I remember running out onto the pitch at Murrayfield and all I was thinking about was my granddad. My mind just wasn't right. I was way off the pace from the start. And so was the rest of the team. We were 19–3 down at half-time and it could have been much, much more. We were that bad.

We were extremely lucky to come away with a losing bonus

point, as a late penalty from Leigh Halfpenny made it only 19–12.

Afterwards the coaches were furious, and rightly so. They asked me why I had been so off the pace, and now, with the funeral to be held that week, I could tell them. I should have told them before. I shouldn't have played.

That death puts things in perspective can be a bit of a cliché, but it is a cliché because it is so true. My granddad's death did put things into perspective for me. It made me realise what is important in life. It instantly told me that my red card was not the earth-shattering incident I maybe saw it as. Yes, it was a massive event in rugby history – and I'll probably be doing a Q&A at a rugby club in west Wales in thirty years' time where we'll still be discussing it – but a red card in sport? Although it was devastating at the time, much worse things have happened.

Just before the Six Nations began I did a live TV interview with Jason Mohammad, the BBC presenter, at my old club in Rhiwbina. I knew that the red card incident would come up, so when it did I decided to nip it in the bud by saying that my granddad's death put it into perspective. It did. And it ended the chat about the red card.

In the same week that my granddad passed away, there was some further tragic news. Sue Evans, wife of Huw, the WRU's official photographer and mum to Ben, Sophie, James and Sam, passed away at the age of just fifty-five. She had battled so bravely against lung cancer, but when I saw a tweet from Angela Rickard, the WRU masseuse who shares a house in Penarth with

Ben, saying that her thoughts were with Ben, I feared the worst. I texted Angela and she gave me the terrible news. I texted Ben. I really felt for him and his family. He is such a good lad who mixes in really well with all of us, and the boys look after him almost like a little brother, taking him under their wing when they go out.

Our next Blues game was on 23 December against Newport Gwent Dragons at home and we wore black armbands and observed a minute's silence in respect of Sue. We won that game quite easily, 28–9 in front of a good crowd of 10,660, with Gavin Henson making his debut for us at full back.

Huw Evans, Ben's dad, has been raising money tirelessly for the Stepping Stones Appeal, which was launched to raise funds for the lung cancer research department at Velindre Cancer Centre. And I too am proud to say that I have become involved in helping Velindre. My grandma was in Velindre and Rachel's mum has also had cancer, which she has overcome. So it is a charity that is close to my heart.

First of all I was asked to be an ambassador and I attended a fashion show for them, before starting their first Winter Walk on 29 December 2011. I also donated items of kit whenever I could for auction. Remarkably they have since asked me to be a patron, alongside the likes of Martyn Williams, Brynmor Williams, James Dean Bradfield of the Manic Street Preachers, and Annelies Krudenier, the young classical singer.

When they announced this at Stepping Stones Rugby Gala dinner on 10 February 2012, three days before we played Scotland in the Six Nations, and with my mum and dad in the audience, Andrew Morris, the head of Velindre Fundraising, said: 'We are delighted to announce that Sam has agreed to become a Velindre Patron – and a very enthusiastic auctioneer on Twitter! We don't usually promote Ambassadors to Patrons so quickly, but Sam's support and enthusiasm over the past eleven months has been absolutely overwhelming and we are delighted that he's accepted.'

I was honoured and privileged to accept. Jonathan Davies (the rugby player who is a bit older than the one with the same name who is in our team at the moment!) is president, and Roy Noble, the broadcaster, is vice-president.

The Blues played the Ospreys on New Year's Day down at the Liberty Stadium, losing 17–12, but I didn't play. I simply had to have a rest. My body was screaming out for it. It was in a world of hurt. My shoulder was still killing me. Usually I can do dumbbell bench press for three reps, with 65kg on each arm. Or I can do five reps at 60kg. Now I was only doing two or three reps at 50kg, such was the pain in my shoulder. I had another cortisone injection. After the Six Nations I had to have another couple more. I reckon by the end of the season I had had seven injections!

But at least now I could have two weeks off and be in some sort of shape to play against Leinster at home in the RaboDirect Pro12 on 7 January.

We lost that game 23–19, but we only had ourselves to blame as we allowed Leinster to rush into a 14–0 lead after just ten minutes, with tries from Sean O'Brien and Rob Kearney.

There were a couple of system errors in the defence and that period just killed us. We tried so hard to get back in the game. And with twenty-two minutes remaining we were only 20–19 behind. Gethin Jenkins had scored a try, Leigh Halfpenny had kicked eleven points, and Dan Parks had dropped a goal. Leigh then uncharacteristically missed a penalty that he would normally get, and not long afterwards Fergus McFadden kicked the vital penalty for Leinster.

Leigh was not to blame for our loss at the Blues. As I said afterwards: 'Leigh kicked brilliantly and it wasn't his fault we lost. We still would have needed more points had Leigh kicked that kick. Credit where it's due, Leinster were very good. They have got some fantastic players. The back-row battle felt like an international match because they're so quick on the ball at the breakdown.'

Two days later I had an important appointment in London. Derwyn had told me that it was vital that I attended the Rugby Union Writers' Club Dinner at the Tower Hotel. It was not an event to which I had been before, and I had no idea what to expect. We drove down there and were a little late taking our seats on the *Rugby World* magazine table.

I was shocked when I got there. It was a big do! There were probably 500 people in the room, including any number of rugby legends. Soon the awards began. Richard Parks, the former Wales flanker, was given the RUWC's Special Award for his incredible achievement of completing his 737 challenge – climbing the seven summits, the highest mountains on each of the world's continents, and standing on all three Poles (the

South Pole, the Geographic North Pole and the summit of Everest), all in the space of seven months.

It was an inspirational journey shown to us at the dinner in an inspirational video. Richard then received his award and made a very good speech. As he was doing so, I was thinking: 'What am I going to say if I've won something?' Derwyn hadn't actually told me that I had won something, but it was very much suggested in the way he had insisted that I had to go.

I did win something. I was presented with the Pat Marshall Trophy for the Personality of 2011 by the previous year's winner Maggie Alphonsi. Apparently in the poll I pipped Graham Henry, Thierry Dusautoir and Shane Williams. I have no idea what I said when I received the award, but I hope it made some sort of sense. I was rather overwhelmed, to say the least.

I hope the RUWC don't mind me saying this, but the cup presented for this award is not a glamorous thing. A few people have come round to my house and seen it taking pride of place in my cabinet and have asked what it is. In truth they've asked with a hint of disdain in their voice. I tell them to check the names on it. It is rather prestigious.

And if you will allow me, I'd like to list the names that are on that trophy. These are the people who have won the Pat Marshall Trophy over the years:

1975–76 MERVYN DAVIES (Swansea and Wales)
1976–77 ANDY IRVINE (Heriot's FP and Scotland)
1977–78 GARETH EDWARDS (Cardiff and Wales)

1978–79 JPR WILLIAMS (Bridgend and Wales)

1979–80 BILL BEAUMONT (Fylde and England)

1980–81 JEAN-PIERRE RIVES (Toulouse and France)

1981–82 OLLIE CAMPBELL (Old Belvedere and Ireland)

1982–83 DAVE LOVERIDGE (Taranaki and New Zealand)

1983–84 JIM AITKEN (Gala and Scotland)

1984–85 MICK DOYLE (Ireland coach)

1985–86 JONATHAN DAVIES (Neath and Wales)

1986–87 DAVID KIRK (Auckland and New Zealand)

1987–88 ROBERT NORSTER (Cardiff and Wales)

1988–89 FINLAY CALDER (Stewart's-Melville FP and Scotland)

1989–90 IAN McGEECHAN (Scotland coach)

1990–91 DAVID CAMPESE (NSW and Australia)

1991–92 NICK FARR-JONES (NSW and Australia)

1992–93 BEN CLARKE (Bath and England)

1993–94 FRANCOIS PIENAAR (Transvaal and South Africa)

1994–95 JONAH LOMU (Counties and New Zealand)

1995–96 SEAN FITZPATRICK (Auckland and New Zealand)

1996–97 LAWRENCE DALLAGLIO (Wasps and England)

1997–98 NICK MALLETT (South Africa coach)

1998–99 TIM HORAN (Queensland and Australia)

1999–2000 PAT LAM (Northampton and Samoa)

2000–01 MARTIN JOHNSON (Leicester and England)
2001–02 JONNY WILKINSON (Newcastle and
    England)
2002–03 MARTIN JOHNSON (Leicester and England)
2003–04 ROBERT HOWLEY (Wasps and Wales)
2004–05 GARETH THOMAS (Toulouse and Wales)
2005–06 JASON WHITE (Sale and Scotland)
2006–07 JASON ROBINSON (Sale and England)
2007–08 SHANE WILLIAMS (Ospreys and Wales)
2008–09 BRIAN O'DRISCOLL (Leinster and Ireland)
2009–10 MAGGIE ALPHONSI (Saracens and England)
2010–11 SAM WARBURTON (Blues and Wales)

Sam Warburton there as the last name – what was going on? I couldn't believe it. That night I drove home from London a very proud man.

Next up was London Irish away in the Heineken Cup, a match given greater significance by Edinburgh winning away at Racing Metro 92 the night before. Yet again we did not play outstandingly well, but we did enough to win 22–15. And I was lucky to be on the end of our only try after some great work from centre Casey Laulala. Leigh Halfpenny kicked seventeen points.

It was all down to the last group match, at home to Racing Metro 92. As against London Irish the week before, I felt that I had a good game. But, as I said, I'd only had four good games out of eight for the Blues since the World Cup. That was my battered body talking. We're not machines. We just can't keep going relentlessly.

We won the match 36–30, but we did not get a four-try bonus point, and Edinburgh playing at home to London Irish did get a bonus point in their 34–11 win. Alex Cuthbert scored two tries and Lloyd Williams one, but it was not enough as we finished second in our pool. We had to travel to Leinster for a quarter-final in April, while Edinburgh were at home to Toulouse, a match they remarkably won 19–14.

I couldn't play in Dublin because of injury. We lost 34–3.

But that was still a long way off. The Six Nations was now looming.

And so, leaving at 4.30am after that Racing Metro 92 match, we embarked on a trip to our favourite country.

9

Ireland Tipped at the Post

We were off to Poland for a week's training before the Six Nations. Not to Spala, but to Gdansk this time and the Cetniewo camp. The good news was that it wasn't quite as bad as the camps in Spala. This facility in Gdansk, overlooking the sea, was much more modern, even if the outside temperature was rather different from that of the summer. It was about minus 10°C, with a wind chill factor of minus 13°C most of the time.

This had to be different. There could not be the same intensity and ferocity of training that we had experienced in the summer, simply because we had to use the cryotherapy chambers at first just to recover from the games we had played that weekend.

The Blues had played on the Sunday, as had the Ospreys out in Biarritz, where they had lost 36–5. The Scarlets had beaten Castres away (16–13) on the Saturday, and in the Amlin Challenge Cup the Newport Gwent Dragons had defeated Prato at home by 45–16 on the same day.

Players were arriving in Gdansk at different times, and in very different states of fitness. Gethin Jenkins had damaged knee ligaments in the Blues match, and he stayed at home while the rest of the Blues players travelled. That was a real blow because Gethin had been in superb form. He missed the first match of the campaign against Ireland but returned to play in all four remaining games.

Rhys Priestland (knee) and Dan Lydiate (ankle) both suffered injuries in their regions' European matches that weekend, and Jamie Roberts had not played for us at the Blues since before Christmas with a knee injury. And it was thought then that we would be without second rows Alun Wyn Jones and Luke Charteris (who had had operations on toe and wrist respectively) for the whole Six Nations campaign. That did not turn out to be the case. Alun Wyn returned for the third match of the campaign, against England at Twickenham, and Luke was on the bench for the two final games against Italy and France.

Stephen Jones was not in the original thirty-five-man squad, but later joined us out in Poland because of some worry over the injury to Rhys Priestland, as well as the fact that James Hook had to return to Perpignan, along with all the other players based in England and France (Mike Phillips, Lee Byrne,

Craig Mitchell, Rhys Gill and Andy Powell) because IRB regulations only allowed them to be with us for three days.

I was not out in Poland for the whole time either. I had to fly back to London on the Tuesday with Alan Phillips and Warren Gatland for the RBS Six Nations launch on Wednesday 25 January at the Hurlingham Club.

We got to the hotel in Chelsea on the Tuesday evening and Warren asked me if I would like to go with him to a meeting with Paddy O'Brien, then the IRB's Referees Manager, and other officials, as well as coaches from the other nations. It was basically a meeting for O'Brien to stress what referees were looking for and what they would focus on in the upcoming tournament. O'Brien said it was going to be no different from the World Cup, where they had been asked to focus on the scrum, maul, offside lines at the breakdown, general foul play and, of course, the tackle.

Ah, the tackle. That was the last item they talked about, and when it came to it there was a little bit of hesitation among O'Brien and his colleagues. I could hear them whispering to each other. They were saying, 'We better not play that,' and in the bottom of their screen I could see an image in which a tackle was being made by a player in a red shirt on one in a blue shirt. I wonder who that was?

There was quite a bit of sniggering going on around the room. I laughed and said to Paddy, 'I don't mind if you play it.' But they didn't. Paddy said, 'I think you've all seen that tackle a hundred times.'

It had been a long day that had begun with a tough training

session in Gdansk and ended with yet another reminder of my tackle on Vincent Clerc. I was starving. The bill was on the WRU surely? Is ordering three main courses on room service too much? I didn't think so. Alan Phillips did. 'What on earth were you doing eating all that food last night?' he asked the next morning when glancing at my room bill.

There were representatives from each of the six nations at the Hurlingham Club. There were the captains from Ireland (Paul O'Connell), Scotland (Ross Ford), Italy (Sergio Parisse), France (Thierry Dusautoir) and Wales (me), while England hadn't decided upon their skipper at that stage so they sent Northampton's Tom Wood, who unfortunately ended up missing the whole tournament because of a toe injury.

It was another long day with endless photos and interviews with TV, radio and the written press, but it was a good opportunity to chat with those players as we spent most of the day together. They are all great blokes. I had a good chat with Tom, because there was something I wanted to ask him: 'Does anyone ever tell you you look like me?'

The reason I asked was because when I had been on holiday in Portugal with Rachel before the Barbarians match in the summer of 2011, a chap had come up to me and asked, 'Are you Tom Wood?' He was an Australian guy who was clearly keen on rugby. I'm certainly too shy just to say, 'No, I'm Sam Warburton.' He asked if I played rugby, and I told him that I did and that I played for Cardiff Blues. Eventually he got my name out of me.

Tom said to me: 'Funny you should say that, but when we (Northampton) played against you (the Blues) in the Heineken Cup, there were even Blues fans coming up to me saying, "Sam, can I have your autograph, please?"'

I'm not sure what the Wales boys made of my being away for a couple of days from Poland. Yes, I missed some training, but it meant I had to make four flights in seven days. That is never ideal. Some of the journalists at the Hurlingham Club asked me about how my absence was being viewed. 'Every cloud has a silver lining,' I joked. 'The boys are probably spewing as we speak!' As it happened, the Thursday was a day off for the squad, so I did extra training that day to make up for what I had missed. That way I didn't feel too guilty.

I got back to the camp in Gdansk late on the Wednesday night, and I tried to be quiet as I crept into the room I was sharing with Dan Lydiate. I thought he was asleep, but suddenly he jumped up and shouted, 'Where have you been? I've been worried sick about you!' We both burst out laughing. We really are like an old married couple.

It was so cold out there. We'd have to be up at 5.45am every day when it was still pitch black, and we'd need five layers of clothing to walk through the snow to the team room, where we'd weigh in and have swab tests to collect saliva for testosterone readings. By 6.30am we'd be in the gym, but we were not necessarily doing hard training. Instead we were doing specific, often unusual, exercises, like working on our running technique or focusing on specific muscle areas, either prehabbing or rehabbing.

Refuse to be Denied

Most of us arrived in Gdansk feeling very stiff and sore after the recent games, but the positive effects of the cryotherapy chambers were there for all to see. We used them on the Monday and it speeded up everyone's recovery to the extent that we were able to train fully a day earlier than we would normally have been expected to. Most players were doing two cryotherapy sessions a day, but some of us who were carrying niggles or more serious injuries were doing three sessions. It was brilliant for players like Dan, Jamie and Rhys, and it noticeably speeded up their recoveries. It certainly made me feel a lot fresher, and my knee and shoulder felt so much better.

The chambers were much less claustrophobic than those in Spala. There it was like being locked in a horrible dark freezer. In Gdansk the windows were larger and there was much more lighting. It was altogether more hi-tech. They had a screen outside so they could see exactly how we were behaving inside, and there was a speaker inside, over which they would play some dodgy Polish music, but also speak to you and let you know how long was left in your session. That naturally had its benefits, but there was one session when the temperature was at its coldest (minus 150°C), and Bradley Davies, waiting outside, decided to count down from sixty for the last minute. It was torture. But it was also quite funny.

By the end of the week the training had become quite hard again. There was one session down on the beach that will linger in the memory for a long time. Sand is usually appealing, but not when the temperature is minus 10°C! It was a brutal session. The cold makes breathing so difficult, but we just ran and ran. This was a mental challenge as much as a physical one. We were then crawling on our elbows, doing 'down and ups', and then more running. The faces on some of the locals who were walking their dogs on the beach were priceless. I don't think they could believe how mad we were. I had four layers on, with gloves and a beanie hat, and I was still cold at the finish.

It was after this that there was a magical call from our conditioner John Ashby. No wonder we all like him so much. We'd finished the session and there was the usual shaking of hands and back slapping as recognition of how hard everyone had worked, as well as the fact that we were all in it together. But it was time to get back to the resort as quickly as we could, and get back into the warm. And there, waiting for us at the resort, was John, with a huge mug of tea for each of us. What a man!

In general, although everything was a little rushed and not everyone could do everything, we tried to recreate the same environment and spirit we had engendered in Spala. We wanted things to be competitive, but we wanted them to be professional and structured. I think we work best as a team when we are given a strict schedule. We know what we are doing then and we will stick to it. And it was not long before the same sort of feeling that we had had in the summer camps returned. We were back together again.

*

The 'Hypertrophy Club' still took place most evenings at around 8pm, just as it had in Spala. There were also some excellent strongman circuit sessions inside, using sandbags in a room that only had mats on the floor. There were obviously plenty of rugby sessions too; there was an all-weather pitch, for which they had a special machine to clear the snow quickly.

The Poland national team were there, and they asked if they could do some training against us. They were huge. The only Polish player I know is Greg Kacala, the back-rower who played for Cardiff in the late nineties and early Millennium. He was huge, and still is, because we saw him during the summer camps in Spala when he came to see Dan Baugh, whom he played with at Cardiff.

We were looking at this Polish team and thinking: 'This is going to be a recipe for disaster. They are just going to try to take our heads off if we train against them.' But we did eventually agree to do some line-outs and scrummages. And it actually went well. We totally dominated them at the scrummages, just to show that it is not all about size. Our boys were too smart for them. But hopefully they learned from their experiences.

We had definitely learned from our experiences in Poland. As the summer camps had before the World Cup, this trip gave us a mental edge going into the Six Nations. It gave us confidence that we had been out there in the cold, putting in the hard graft. The coaches are always saying that we are training harder than anyone else, and in the World Cup, whenever we were in a dark place during a game, someone might say,

'Remember Poland.' And that happened again during the Six Nations. We always had those valuable points of reference.

We were confident going into that first match against Ireland in Dublin. Not that anyone else seemed to be. It was just like the World Cup quarter-final. Yes, their provinces were doing well in Europe, and yes, we had injury problems. But we felt that we had excellent cover in all the positions. We were thinking, 'Hang on, we've beaten Ireland the last two times we've played them. How come we're not favourites?' It annoyed me that nobody was talking us up. Yet the last of our home games, against France, was already sold out. Didn't that mean that everyone was anticipating it to be the Championship-winning game?

I thought that as we had done so well at the World Cup, we would be installed as favourites. I wanted us to have that pressure. You could argue that statistically France were favourites because they had made it to the World Cup final, but they had only just scraped past us when we had fourteen men. With all due respect, they were not scaring us at that stage.

We didn't want to be the underdogs. We wanted people to fancy our chances. I didn't think it was arrogant to say we wanted to win the Championship. I am sure most teams were saying the same thing. If we wanted to become the top nation in the world, then surely winning the Six Nations should be a realistic target?

As I told the press: 'All the players definitely want to be part of a winning Six Nations Championship. I'm yet to be part of one of those, so I'd love to experience that. I've only been involved in two Six Nations campaigns and I loved both of them. This year is a good one because we have got three home games and every game at the Millennium Stadium is fantastic.'

We had spoken about the importance of this game. We knew what a massive statement it would send out if we won. From day one the target was to win the Grand Slam. The coaches had urged us not to look too far ahead, and there were times during the campaign when I would say that we couldn't mention the two dreaded words beginning with 'G' and 'S', but the truth was that amongst ourselves we had said that we wanted to win it. That's the exuberance and confidence of youth for you. So many of us have not been through the bad times.

At the same time we knew that it would be very different from being out in New Zealand, where all eyes were on the All Blacks. All eyes would be on us now. That was going to bring a slightly different pressure. Maybe we were going to have to shut ourselves away from the media more than normal, and not watch too many post-match discussions on TV or pore over the papers.

And we were going to have to be careful about our off-field behaviour. That's why I sat down with Matthew Rees and a couple of others before the campaign and came up with a plan regarding alcohol. We didn't want any distracting stories, so after home games no one was allowed to go out in Cardiff. If players wanted a quiet beer they could have it at the hotel bar, and that was the same at away games. I'm afraid that these days going out with fans straight after the game, especially in the middle of a campaign, is a definite no. Of course, 99 per cent of fans are supportive, but there is that 1 per cent who might want to cause trouble. We just can't risk it. Unless we've won the Grand Slam, of course. That is different.

The side eventually selected included ten players who had started when we beat Ireland in Wellington: Alex Cuthbert for the retired Shane Williams was an obvious change, while in the forwards Dan Lydiate, Gethin Jenkins, Alun Wyn Jones and Luke Charteris were all out injured, to be replaced by Ryan Jones, Rhys Gill, Bradley Davies and Ian Evans.

See what I mean about quality replacements? Everyone was soon talking about Alex Cuthbert. That's how good he is. Bradley Davies is a seasoned, excellent international. And we wanted to target Ireland at the scrummage and Rhys Gill loves his scrummaging, so that was not a problem. Ian Evans turned out to be one of the players of the Six Nations, and Ryan Jones was many observers' player of the year once the domestic season had finished. Matthew Rees had been ruled out of contention with a calf injury, meaning Huw Bennett would win his fiftieth cap; Rhys Priestland and Jamie Roberts had both recovered sufficiently from their knee injuries to play.

Matthew's injury also meant that I was definitely going to be captain. I was comfortable with that now, as I'd said before the Australia game in Cardiff. But I wasn't taking it for granted, that is for sure. When asked about it earlier I'd said, 'I've had no indication what's going to happen. Matthew was captain for the last Six Nations campaign and did a brilliant job. It was only bad luck why he didn't end up being captain for the World Cup. If I did it as a temporary thing I could completely understand that.'

In the World Cup we had played with no fear and never once did we go into our shells. That was my message to the players again now: no fear. But we had to be mindful of how Ireland would be thinking. I told the players that if I was in Ireland's shoes, I'd be devastated at the loss in the quarter-final of the World Cup and the defeat in Cardiff the previous season after Mike Phillips' controversial try. 'With those two games at their back of their minds,' I said to them, 'we've got to expect the first twenty minutes to be the toughest you've ever experienced in an international match. It will be one of those ramped-up Irish performances like they produced against England in the last match of the 2011 Six Nations. If we don't turn up in those first twenty minutes, it could be a very difficult afternoon.'

I was expecting it to be physical. I even had a special new red head guard to wear. It was obvious that I had become much more of a target at the breakdown after the World Cup, and I was getting a lot of elbows and knees. In some games I was really getting smashed and would have headaches for a couple of days afterwards. So I started to wear a head guard for the Blues.

I have a confession to make here. I can be a little bit dozy sometimes. Anyone who knows me well will read that and laugh. They might laugh a bit more when I say that I had not actually tried my new red head guard on before the match. So there I was lining up for the anthem against Ireland with my head guard in my hand. The anthems finished and I gathered the team around in a huddle. I put my head guard onto my head and tried to pull it down. It got stuck on the top of my head! I had to run to the side of the pitch and throw it off.

I didn't get any nasty bangs to the head in that game and so I haven't worn one since. The main reason is that whenever I do wear one I really struggle to hear. I can't hear what the referee is saying, and in my position that is a serious problem. Mind you, I'm not too keen on 'cauliflower ears' either, and it's not a look Rachel would go for, so I might have to wear one again some day!

If it's honesty time about being forgetful, then perhaps I should also say that I forgot my suit for the after-match function in Ireland. We were sitting on the plane at Cardiff Airport, waiting to fly to Dublin, when it dawned on me. The captain, who has to make a speech at the after-dinner function, had forgotten his suit.

Toby Faletau was sitting next to me. 'I've forgotten my suit, Tobes,' I said.

'That is going to be a mental fine,' he laughed.

'Or Thumper is going to go mental,' I thought.

As it happened, our team manager Alan Phillips was sitting right behind us. There was no point beating about the bush. 'Thump, I've forgotten my suit, mate,' I said.

'You clown,' he replied. Or at least that was the repeatable bit of his response. 'You'll have to ask one of the other players if you can borrow their suit and they'll have to stay back at the hotel,' he said.

Ah, my man was sitting right next to me. You won't find a quieter man in rugby. You won't find a man less at home at a function.

'Tobes, how do you fancy missing the after-match function tomorrow?' I said. His eyes lit up. 'If you lend me your suit, you can stay in the hotel,' I added.

He smiled the smile of a very happy man. I think the words 'golden ticket' might have been mentioned. I had a deal.

But you know what happened? When I said earlier that I did not get any bad bangs to the head in the game, I did not mention that I got a nasty bang to my leg. In fact I had such a bad dead leg that, like Alex Cuthbert who'd had a bang to the head, I did not come out for the second half. And that meant that after the game I had to ice my leg. Prav Mathema, our physio, is adamant that icing must override all other duties after the game, so I wasn't allowed to go to the after-match function. Ryan Jones had to speak instead.

And Toby? He didn't go to the function either. He was 'injured' apparently, even though, as I've said, he doesn't get too many injuries. His mind was set that he wasn't going to that function, I reckon.

So myself, Tobes, Justin Tipuric (who had replaced me and hurt his ankle during the second half) and Huw Bennett sat in the hotel icing our various injuries while the function went on. I asked the waiter if he had any chocolate, but unfortunately he hadn't. So we all had steak and chips.

When the rest of the players came back there was a real buzz in the air, just as there had been in the changing rooms afterwards when Gethin Jenkins, our music man, had put on his 'winning' compilation of eighties classics, with songs like 'Don't Stop Believing' by Journey.

We had beaten Ireland 23–21, and I could already sense a feeling that something special was brewing. There was so much confidence about everyone. We had talked about how important this game was, and to have got the result we wanted brought with it a real sense of achievement and expectation of more to come. Things can just snowball when you win.

It was a remarkable match. Sitting on the bench I could not watch at the end. It was just like the France semi-final all over again for me: I was hoping and praying that we would get a penalty to win the game. In Auckland it just hadn't happened. The penalty had come, but Leigh Halfpenny's kick from near halfway dropped agonisingly short. Here in Dublin it also came, albeit in controversial circumstances.

There was about a minute to go, with us trailing 21–20, when Mike Phillips popped a ball to Ian Evans in the middle of the field. Stephen Ferris came in with the tackle, and upended Ian, or 'Ianto' as we call him. It was a tip tackle. Ferris was yellow carded and we were obviously awarded a penalty about 30 metres out in front of the posts.

Up stepped Leigh. He had taken over the kicking duties from Rhys Priestland earlier, because Rhys was not having one of his better days. As captain I was off the field when that happened, but it wouldn't have been a decision that I would have had to make. Neil Jenkins, our kicking coach, would have been the one to make that call.

Cool as can be, Leigh nailed it. We were 23–21 up with only seconds to go. We secured the restart and Rhys booted the ball into touch. We had won! Andy Powell, who had not been used as a replacement, screamed at the top of his voice and ran across the pitch in jubilation. He was going mad.

When we did the team debrief afterwards Warren stopped the tape and said, 'Spot the crazy blonde guy ...' and we all had a good giggle at Andy.

I was so pleased for Leigh. I shook his hand with real feeling afterwards. I know how much he cares. He had been devastated after the France match, and he had taken this opportunity to exorcise his demons from that match. He really does beat himself up over things sometimes. I remember after a Cardiff Blues match once when Richie Rees went up to him and said: 'Don't worry, it's only a game of rugby, Pence.' That's his nickname by the way, 'Pence'. Come on, you can work that out. Some people actually call him 'Pens' now.

Leigh practises so hard. At the Blues he is always late for lunch because he is staying out doing extra kicking. Apparently he does a lot more back down in Gorseinon too. He is a great pro. And he wants to be the main goalkicker. For a while he was just the long-distance specialist, but he wants to be more than that.

Should Ferris have got a yellow card? I don't think so. But it was a penalty, and as a result I think we deserved to win.

When we kept the ball I thought we looked really good. And the truth is, as Warren said afterwards, we were probably only at 70 per cent of our capabilities. We realised that when we studied the video of the match. There were occasions when players had worked really hard to achieve certain situations and then they had been wasted. But we did create a lot of opportunities. We could have scored four tries, because Ryan Jones was adamant that he'd scored one in the first half that was disallowed. The final result looked as if we'd only just scraped home because of that penalty, but it should be remembered that we had created that opportunity as well.

As well as Ferris's, there was another tackle that caused controversy. It was after sixty-five minutes and I will admit that I did not see it live. I only saw it on a TV monitor as I was being interviewed after the match. Immediately it did not look good. It was by Bradley Davies on Donnacha Ryan and it was a long way off the ball. Bradley had become angry when Ryan took out Adam Jones at a ruck and had then picked him up and dumped him head first.

Referee Wayne Barnes hadn't see the incident and so had asked touch judge Dave Pearson for help. Pearson advised that Bradley should be given a yellow card. He was very lucky. It was much worse than my tackle on Vincent Clerc. It should have been a red card.

Everyone agreed with that afterwards, I think. Warren was certainly very honest about it when he spoke to the media and when he spoke to us in the changing room. He simply told Bradley it had been cynical and could have been costly. Bradley knew that. And he paid for it by missing the rest of the Six Nations.

Warren reminded me of the Special Forces guy, Sven, whom I mentioned earlier. Sven told me that in the Forces after combat they always have what's called 'a hot discussion'. When everybody is very emotional – a bit like when you're drunk, I suppose – you can say what went right and what went wrong with brutal honesty. He recommended we did that after matches, and that's exactly what Warren did here. Not that I had prompted him, mind.

Warren was still not happy the following week. The problem with cards was vexing him badly. After Bradley had been sin-binned, Tommy Bowe had scored almost immediately to put Ireland 21–15 ahead. Warren stood up in a team meeting and asked us the question: 'What are we going to do about these cards? ... Do we bring in some sort of punishment of our own? Do we make the player do so many public appearances or school visits, or something like that? What about fines? Say £10,000? £20,000? £30,000 maybe?' The room fell silent. George North was sitting next to me and he nudged me with his knee. Everyone was thinking the same thing – we're not footballers after all.

Usually in that situation you can count on one man to say what everyone else wants to say. Up stood Gethin Jenkins. 'I don't think we should do that, Warren,' he said. After that meeting 'Melon' has rarely been so popular: 'Thanks Mel, you saved us there, mate. You're a legend.' And as it was, nothing formal was introduced. Maybe Warren had scared us enough with his threat.

But the tip tackle debate had reared its head again. 'Is the reaction to them getting a little out of hand?' I asked in the *Daily Telegraph* column that I wrote throughout the Six Nations:

I think it might be, if I'm honest. Obviously I'm not advocating dangerous tackles in the game, but the problem is that everyone is looking for consistency, and I don't think there is an answer that can be written in black and white. Every case is different. There should be more interpretation of individual circumstances.

Let's take these three tackles. Firstly mine in the World Cup on Vincent Clerc. I had to make a decision in about half a second as to which man to take – either the scrum-half or winger coming round from a line-out. I took the winger Clerc. It was a legitimate hit without malice. He went flying up in the air. I panicked and let him go. Result? A red card.

Next let's take my teammate Bradley Davies' tackle on Donnacha Ryan last Sunday in Dublin. I'll admit that I didn't see it live. I was, of course, on the bench having departed at half-time with a dead leg, and spent most of the last quarter with my head in my hands. I just couldn't watch because it was so tense. I saw the tackle for the first time when I was about to do a post-match television interview and was shown it on the monitor. I knew immediately that Bradley was in trouble. It was so far away from the ball. In that instance you just don't have a leg to stand on, if you'll excuse the pun. Bradley looked like he'd got irritated, and it was an act of aggression that did look malicious. He didn't spear Ryan into the ground, but he did pick him up and dump him. It was a tip tackle in my view. Result? Upon the touch-judge's recommendation, a yellow card. Nobody could have argued with a red card. And now Bradley has been given a seven-week ban.

He was gutted enough anyway, as we always make a big thing about yellow cards. They have cost us before and Bradley's could have cost us here. A few years ago we would probably have lost that game, but we think that we are in such good physical shape that we got away with it. It's hard because sometimes in a game you do see red (again excusing the pun!), if, say, someone puts in a cheap shot, but you think about revenge for a split second then get on with the game. You just have to these days. Discipline is too important.

Finally there is Stephen Ferris' tackle on Ian Evans, also last Sunday. Ferris knew which man he was going to tackle. His too was a legitimate hit, but he came in at an angle. There was no malicious intent, but Ian did go up in the air. And Ferris did bring him back down. Result? Yellow card.

All these tackles fall into the same bracket, yet they are all so different. Accidents sometimes do happen on a rugby field, and I think we need to be careful in handing out cards so easily. Ferris' yellow was harsh in my opinion. But I do think the penalty was fair.

What pleased me most was the players' attitude after Bradley was sin-binned. They were so determined. It was as if they were saying: 'It was pointless going on all those trips to Poland if we give up now.' There was a steely determination that they weren't going to accept a respectable loss away from home.

And then there was George North. What a game he had. Mike Phillips was made the official man of the match, and he did have a fine game, but he admitted himself that George probably should have got the award. Warren said afterwards in the changing room that George had been 'world-class', and I don't think you'll find anyone who would disagree with that. It was an amazing performance. He scored a try in the second half with just five minutes remaining that brought us back to 21–20. It was sheer power that brought him that try, with Irish defenders seemingly scattered everywhere.

Twenty minutes earlier he had produced a moment of magic to put Jon Davies through for his second try (although Jon still had a bit to do in fairness to him!). Justin Tipuric had won a line-out at the tail and, with Jamie Roberts making a decoy run, George had come steaming into the line off Rhys Priestland. First he had gone outside Gordon D'Arcy, and then he had run over Fergus McFadden. As Jonathan Sexton came across to make the tackle and Andrew Trimble came in to help, George flicked the ball out of the back of his right hand – the 'cat flap' as it has become known – to Jon. It was an amazing piece of skill. In that respect we shouldn't forget Rhys Priestland's brilliant pass out of the double tackle from Mike Ross and Tommy Bowe for Jon to score his first try after just thirteen minutes. Remarkably, I'm not even sure George's 'cat flap' was his best piece of skill on the day. There was one take of a high ball above his head with three Irish chasers bearing down on him that I thought was outstanding.

Sitting and watching the second half I was marvelling at him just like everyone else in the crowd. When George did his 'cat flap' I celebrated initially, but then I turned to Ryan Chambers, our sports scientist, and Ashley Beck, the Ospreys centre who was 23rd man for this match, and said: 'People forget that he is only nineteen years of age.'

He is unbelievable. I've said it before and so have many others now, and it's always been meant as a compliment, but he's a freak. No matter how often someone trains, there will still be things George can do that that person can't. Our Dutch sprint coach, Frans Bosch, reckons George's 10-metre acceleration is as good as the top sprinters, but what he can't understand is that those sprinters are 80–90kg in weight, while George weighs 110kg and he still shifts as quickly. Mind you, all of our backline are huge these days. I think they were 9kg a man heavier than Ireland in this match, and most of them – certainly George, Jamie Roberts, Jon Davies and Alex Cuthbert – are heavier than my 103kg. And they're all much quicker than me!

There would have been quite a few people who were quicker than me in the week after that Ireland game. My dead leg just wouldn't ease. We were playing Scotland at home a week after the Ireland match on Sunday 12 February, and it was a race against time to get myself fit.

It wasn't just one incident that caused the injury. I'd taken a blow a couple of times on the same spot on the side of my thigh. It was basically a bruise. And it's not very heroic to come off with a bruise. I was getting stick about that from the old-school boys like Dan Baugh. He reckoned that in his day they just stretched off a dead leg and carried on playing. I did point out to him: 'Yes, but in your day, people were only 12-stone on the pitch!' It was a lot worse than it sounded. Basically what happens with a dead leg is that a blood vessel is ruptured and blood is released into the muscle and develops into a haematoma. It's painful, let me tell you.

I tried everything I could to be fit for the Scotland match. I was helped by the fact that we had decided to acquire a mobile cryotherapy chamber, like the ones they use in cycling's Tour de France. After our experiences in Poland the idea was put to the players, and we were all really keen. As I've said, the chamber can give us an extra day's training during the week when we might otherwise be recovering. And at minus 160°C it's even colder than those in Poland. It's like a stand-up sunbed, a cylinder-type shape and with only one man able to go in at a time. We queue up, have our three and a half minutes and walk back out. You are in it up to your shoulders, so it just does your torso and lower half. I was using it two or three times a day; even on my day off I drove up to the Vale Hotel, jumped in it and then went home.

All week Mark Davies, the physio, worked hard on breaking up the haematoma. I was also seeing Andy McCann. I'm of the opinion that a positive mental attitude can aid healing, and Prav Mathema, the other physio, supports that view. Andy asked me how I perceived the haematoma on my leg. He wanted me to imagine it being broken up. For some reason the first thing that came into my mind was an onion bhaji. The Juboraj Indian restaurant in Rhiwbina is our favourite family destination for food, and I just love the onion bhajis there. So I know this might sound a bit random and strange, but that's what I did: I imagined that my haematoma was an onion bhaji

211

from the Juboraj, and by concentrating hard on it I tried to break it up.

I so wanted to play against Scotland. I want to play every international Wales play. You never know what is around the corner, so my philosophy is that I must do everything I can to try to play in every game, whoever it is against.

My dad also wanted me to play. He and Mum love the Six Nations. They love being in the Millennium Stadium watching me play. So Dad was on the phone all week. 'How's your leg?' he would ask.

On Monday I was saying, 'It's only 50–50 at the moment, sorry.' I could hear his disappointment on the other end of the phone. He'd phone then on the Tuesday. 'I reckon it's 80–20 in favour of being fit today,' I'd say to him, and I could hear his joy at that news. By the end of the week my mum was phoning me and saying, 'Your dad doesn't want to keep asking you, but how is your leg?'

The truth was that it wasn't great. It had improved, but had it improved enough to play a Test? It was still painful when I tried to bend it past 90 degrees. And it was painful to touch. When the physios just tapped it, it hurt. I was thinking: 'What happens when a 17-stone Scottish forward slams into it with his shoulder?' I hadn't trained all week, and I couldn't lie on it at night. It was just throbbing all the time. We tried using compression bandages, and I was using the 'Game Ready' ice machine every two hours, but progress was slow.

The problem was that Justin Tipuric was definitely out with his ankle injury, and we didn't have another specialist openside flanker in the squad. The Scarlets Aaron Shingler had been called into the squad, and he had trained all week at seven, even though he had never played in that position before, not even for his region. But he had been having a really good season, having become a regular in their side, either on the blind-side flank or in the second row. He'd had an excellent Heineken Cup, scoring three tries, including a stunning length-of-the-field effort against Castres.

I was named in the starting line-up to face Scotland. As were Gethin Jenkins and Dan Lydiate, who both returned from injury to replace Rhys Gill, who had done really well in Ireland, and Ryan Jones, who moved from flanker to second row to replace the suspended Bradley Davies. The Scarlets second row Lou Reed was named on the bench and came on to win his first cap. I was asked by the press whether I thought it was a risk picking me. 'Maybe,' I said. 'Because I haven't done any contact. That's the risk we've got to take. I'm not really going to think like that. I'm just going to go out and not try and restrict myself. I'm going to play as hard as I can and see what happens. Because (Justin) Tipuric has been ruled out, I have had to be quite cautious and make sure I don't knock it again. It's not too bad. I haven't taken contact on it. I can trot around. There's still another forty-eight hours to the game, and the progression I've made so far in the last few days ... well, that's why I feel so positive about it. I think I will be all right.

'I have had it before and been out for six weeks, but credit to the physios here for the way they managed me during the first two days. I was up every two hours at night, so credit to the medical staff that I have come back so quickly. If we hadn't managed it so well early in the week, I would probably have been out of this game.'

If there was doubt about my participation, there was no such doubt as to what sort of performance we needed against Scotland. It had to be convincing. They had been unlucky in their first match at home to England when they lost 13–6, despite having numerous chances to win. We watched that game in our hotel in Dublin and I could share the Scots' frustrations. They had a 'try' from Greg Laidlaw disallowed, as he went for the ball at the same time as England's Ben Youngs; I thought it was a try.

But I said: 'Scraping through against Scotland will not be good enough. We have got to play well and have an impressive win. The World Cup was one step forward, and I think beating Ireland away was a big statement, but there is no point doing that and then struggling at home. We need to put in a strong performance defensively and in attack.'

I knew it wouldn't be easy. At Cardiff Blues we'd played Edinburgh twice in the Heineken Cup and I'd seen how good a player back-rower David Denton was. He'd made his first Test start against England and had played so well that he was made man of the match. I remember after our first match against Edinburgh I'd said to Gethin Jenkins: 'He is one hell of a player. He's got to be in Scotland's Six Nations squad.' He was a real handful, a powerful ball-carrier and a tremendous competitor at the breakdown.

I was still struggling to be fit. At the team run on the

Saturday I thought it best if I spoke to Aaron and told him that there was a good chance he might be playing. He needed that time to prepare himself mentally.

I wasn't ruled out officially until the Sunday morning, because we were just hoping against hope that there might be some dramatic improvement overnight. It was so disappointing when the decision was made after a fitness test on the Sunday morning.

I was still with the team. I travelled to the stadium on the team bus and I was in the changing room beforehand. My name was even still on the individual banners that are put on the pitch before the match. That was so galling. I was asked if I wanted to sit on the bench alongside the replacements and management staff during the game, but I didn't feel as if that would be right. There was nothing I could offer down there. Ryan Jones was captain for the day, and there was so much experience in the side that it wasn't my place to be butting in. I left them to it and watched the match from a hospitality box with Matthew Rees.

We won 27–13. I thought Aaron did really well. We had a few issues at the breakdown in the first half, which ended with the scores level at 3–3, but that was mainly because Ross Rennie was having a brilliant game for Scotland.

We lost George North just before half-time with an ankle injury, and he was replaced by James Hook, who went to full back, with Leigh Halfpenny moving to the wing. And Huw Bennett did not appear for the second half, replaced by Ken Owens.

Refuse to be Denied

When we were given a sniff just after half-time, we took it. We did more than that actually. We blew Scotland away. We were 27–6 ahead in no time and the game was over. First Scotland made a mistake from the kick-off, and it was just the sort of position in their half we were looking for. Hooky fed Alex Cuthbert, who ran through Laidlaw to score. Minutes later Nick de Luca was in the sin bin for tackling Jon Davies without the ball after Jon had hacked ahead. And we took advantage as Leigh scored. He was given the final pass by Cuthbert, but Gethin Jenkins and Dan Lydiate had done some great work in the build-up. Dan had a magnificent match on his return and was duly named man of the match. What a comeback.

Scotland then went down to thirteen men momentarily when Rory Lamont was given a yellow card for a tackle on Hooky from a blatantly off-side position. De Luca returned from the sin bin, but we scored again through Leigh, who wrapped around from open to blind at a scrummage. Leigh, taking over the kicking duties throughout, converted all three tries and kicked two penalties to finish with twenty-two points overall. Scotland did score a try through Laidlaw, who converted it to add to his two earlier penalties, but in the end it was a comfortable win.

We could even afford to lose Gethin Jenkins to the sin bin three minutes from full time, when he did not roll away from a tackle. And he might have mentioned afterwards that he did not think it was worth £30,000 . . .

10

Twickenham Triple Crown

I very nearly didn't make the England game either. There were thirteen days between that and the Scotland victory, but my dead leg refused to ease. I didn't do any contact work in the lead up to the Twickenham match, and the only session I did other than the Friday team run was on the Thursday, and then I only did about twenty minutes before missing the contact section.

Little wonder that the boys were already calling me 'Team-run Warby' and talking about 'Captainitis', because it seems that whoever is made captain then picks up an injury and doesn't do much training. It happened to Matthew Rees, and it has happened to Ryan Jones and Gethin Jenkins. I remember one training session during the summer, which I was about to sit out, and in which Matthew, Ryan and Gethin were about to take part. 'You training, Warby?' they asked.

'No,' I replied.

'Ah, that's standard. Warby's not training.'

At that moment Bradley Davies appeared, and never one to miss an opportunity of a quip, turned to Matthew, Ryan and Gethin and said, 'Look at you three all having to dig in and train properly now you're not captain.' Ah, all good banter.

What didn't amuse me so much was the mentality of so many observers ahead of the England game: they weren't happy that we were favourites; they preferred us to be underdogs. I found that really strange. We were favourites and we deserved to be. Yes, England had beaten both Scotland and Italy away from home, results we would have been happy with, but they had admitted they hadn't been at their best. We had played well in beating Ireland and Scotland. We'd also had an excellent World Cup. Why couldn't we be favourites?

But still our poor record at Twickenham was being trotted out: that we had won only once in our last thirteen Tests there, and that the average score had been something like 36–14 against us. How many of our players had played in all of those matches? I remember saying to the team that there were only two statistics that mattered: that we had won there in 2008, when players like Mike Phillips, Adam Jones, Alun Wyn Jones, Ryan Jones, Ian Evans and Gethin Jenkins were involved, and that we had beaten England the last time we had played them (at the Millennium Stadium the previous summer).

It's all about 'on the day'. That's why I don't believe in the history. And I don't understand the Welsh mentality some-times. We need to change it.

I love the attitude in countries like the USA and Australia, where there is such an emphasis on winning. In this country kids are told about participation and enjoyment, which is obviously very important, but I think greater emphasis has got to be placed on winning. That's what we have to change in the UK. We've got to throw that 'underdogs' tag out of the window.

I'm a huge fan of an American conditioning coach called Joe DeFranco. He has trained NFL footballers, as well as boxers and baseball and hockey players. I love how he creates such an elitist environment at his gym. It's all about leader boards and singling people out. You can only change the music if you bench press or squat a certain weight. It's such a great training culture, and it's exactly what we are trying to create in the Wales squad.

We thought we could win at Twickenham and were comfort-able with that mindset. Not that I have the same bitter rivalry that a lot of Welsh people have towards England. It is no secret that I have some English connections. My father is English. One of four children in a family originally from the north of England, he was born in London, where he lived for the first few months of his life before moving to Birmingham, and he was five when he came to live in Cardiff. I have a lot of relatives who still live in the north of England, and my grandmother has a broad Yorkshire accent. My mother was born in Somerset to Welsh parents, and she considers herself very much Welsh. Thanks to my mum, I actually have a double-barrelled surname: Kennedy-Warburton. Now I consider that very English!

That's one reason I only use the surname Warburton these days. I hope it doesn't offend my mum too much, as she clearly wanted to keep her maiden name going, but I felt that it just wouldn't sound right in a Wales team with all those Joneses and Davieses.

Although I never thought about making myself available for England, I did support them during the 2003 World Cup. Jonny Wilkinson was my hero back then. My dad still supports England at football, but he's very much a Wales rugby fan, as he showed by crying tears of joy when we beat England in Cardiff in the World Cup warm-up match. Mind you, my uncle Andrew had come over from Denmark to watch that game, and he wasn't sure which team to support!

Let me say that none of these English connections have anything to do with the fact that I don't sing the Welsh national anthem before matches. I'd been told before the England match that the WRU had received an enormous amount of calls and emails complaining that I don't sing the anthem. And it was clearly still an issue after the Six Nations when I did a Q&A session and was asked this very question. I'm glad to say that my answer received a good round of applause. I just don't feel comfortable singing it, mainly because I am not very good at singing. I've never sung the anthem before a game, even when I was playing through the Wales age-group sides. I did mouth the words before the England match, but even doing that felt uncomfortable.

I know it goes against the Welsh tradition, but I don't really like singing. I prefer to listen to the anthem. In my mind I'm singing the words, and it's during that time that I think about my parents, my brother and sister, my girlfriend, and about how I dreamt about playing for Wales when I was at school. I think of training with Ben on our multigym and about how I had trained all along for this moment. I think about the people who have helped me, like my coaches Gwyn Morris and Bob Newman, and Frank Rees, the headmaster at Llanishen Fach Primary School, who said I must play rugby and went to my parents and said, 'The boy has something.' I use these thoughts as motivation before a match. International rugby is quite an intense environment to be involved in, and I think you just need to do whatever suits you best.

It doesn't mean I'm not patriotic. I will give everything for Wales. When I'm on the pitch in that Welsh jersey, I'm so pumped up, so passionate, giving it 100 per cent every game. I never want to go off during a match. In 2010 against South Africa I broke my jaw after just twenty-four seconds, but I didn't come off until two minutes before the end of the game. I am so proud to be Welsh, and to be playing for Wales; to be standing there while a full Millennium Stadium sings our anthem is an amazing feeling.

I was desperate to beat England. But we knew it was probably going to be the hardest, most physical match of the Championship. It always is against England. You wake up the next morning feeling as if you have been hit by a car.

When we played those two World Cup warm-up matches

against England, it was noticeable how fit we felt in the closing stages. Even when we lost at Twickenham, we finished strongly. And we were certainly confident of our fitness before this match. We lost in Cardiff in the 2011 Six Nations Championship mainly because we weren't as fit then; we just weren't quite there as a side then. As a result I don't think we had the confidence that we had now.

We made three changes from the Scotland game. I came back in to replace Aaron Shingler, Ken Owens replaced the injured Huw Bennett at hooker for his first start (with Matthew Rees still injured as well), and in the second row Alun Wyn Jones made his first appearance of the campaign, taking over from Ryan Jones. That must have been a very tough decision for the management to make, because Ryan had done superbly, but Alun Wyn does run the line-outs and that must have swayed the decision.

We were relaxed in the build-up. I may have been a little too relaxed before we left, because I forgot my suit again. I am just so forgetful sometimes, but as soon as it's time for rugby action, I'm able to switch on very quickly!

Luckily this time I wasn't travelling on the team bus. I'd had a nasty cold all week, as had George North, who had recovered from the ankle injury sustained against Scotland. So to keep us away from the rest of the squad we were driven up to London by our team doctor Professor John Williams. It meant I shared a room with George at our Richmond hotel.

I remembered about my suit just in time, and we did a detour to my house in Thornhill to pick it up before heading onto the M4. George was sitting in the front of the car, and he was so excited. It was like taking a kid to a theme park. Well, he was only nineteen at the time, I suppose! After about an hour he fell asleep. I said to Prof, 'There, I told you it was like having a kid with us!' I couldn't resist taking a photo of him and posting it on Twitter. The only trouble was that I then fell asleep and George got his revenge. I fell asleep with my hand over my bag and George reckoned it looked like I was attempting a 'jackal' in the back seat.

George loves that sort of funny stuff. It was an interesting week for him and his Scarlets colleagues in the Wales team, because Ben Morgan, their Scarlets teammate, was making his first start for England after coming off the bench against Scotland and Italy. He'd done really well in those second-half appearances and we knew he was a serious threat. Before each game we decide upon a 'smoke target' in the opposition. Shaun Edwards, along with the defensive captains Dan Lydiate, Gethin Jenkins and Jamie Roberts, will decide which member of the opposition we really need to 'smoke' when they are attacking. Against England Ben Morgan was the 'smoke target'.

In the week after the game George and I were reviewing the game in the analysis room, and in a camera shot from above we spotted something strange while England were having a team huddle. Ben Morgan was spewing up. How George loved that! He took a photo and sent it to Ben immediately. And he also sent a couple of other photos, entitled 'Before' and 'After', as George ran at Ben and then beat him.

*

We won the match 19–12, and as I said afterwards it was 'one hell of a Test match'. It's probably best if we begin at the end. Did David Strettle score for England right at the death, which would have meant a difficult conversion attempt for Toby Flood to level the scores?

England had been putting us under some serious pressure in those closing moments. They had had a couple of line-outs near our line and had gone very close to scoring. Then the ball was moved right to Flood, who was on as a replacement for Owen Farrell. He threw a long overhead pass off his left hand to Mike Brown, who was on for Ben Foden. Brown gave the ball to Strettle early and the winger went for the corner.

Haring across from the other side of the pitch was Leigh Halfpenny, who hurled himself headfirst at Strettle without any regard for his own safety. It was a heroic tackle, even if it only half-stopped Strettle. It was vital in the circumstances. But poor Leigh did not know where he was afterwards. It was one almighty blow that he took to his head. He was in a right state in the changing rooms, just sitting there staring into space, with doctors checking on him constantly in case he was sick. The rest of us were going mad, but most of us were glancing at Leigh every now and then, and thinking: 'Fair play. He's a hero for what he's done there.'

He had stopped Strettle momentarily as he cut back inside so that Jon Davies could then make a tackle on him. Strettle landed short of the line and then rolled over with Jon wrapped around him, stretching out his arm as he went over the line as

George came across to tackle him too. Strettle and Brown were claiming the try quite confidently.

Steve Walsh was the referee and he had been running across the field in the in-goal area. His view was probably blocked by George and he was not sure whether the ball had been grounded. But he did say to the touch judge Pascal Gauzere, who said he did not have a clear view either, 'I think he was held up but I'm going to have a check.' So it was referred to the television match official Iain Ramage. 'Try or no try?' Walsh asked Ramage. So Ramage had to find conclusive evidence that Strettle had scored.

What a wait that was until Ramage came back to Walsh with his decision. I'll be honest and say that, looking at the big screen in the stadium, it looked like a try. Those screens obviously don't produce the sharpest picture, and you could see that Strettle had gone over the line. I just thought he might have managed to move his wrist to ensure that the ball made some contact with the ground; you have to remember that it only has to make contact for that split second.

So I just made my way towards the posts, expecting a conversion and to get the boys ready to run hard for a charge-down. I remember saying to Mike Phillips: 'We've just got to make sure it's not a draw!' I was praying that it wasn't going to be given, but I thought it would be.

And then Walsh relayed the decision that the game was over. The pictures were inconclusive. I watched them when I went home and 'inconclusive' is definitely the right word. You just can't tell. I think you need a bit of luck if you want to do well in campaigns. We'd had a bit of luck.

225

What a relief! If the end had come normally, we'd have been jumping in the air. I'm not sure I could ever call beating England an anticlimax, but it did feel rather strange after that wait.

I was a little bit disappointed really. As I said immediately afterwards: 'We didn't play well at all today.' I knew we hadn't actually played as well as we had in the first two games. It wasn't a vintage performance by any means. We didn't play enough territory, as we tried to play a little bit too much and run it back too often. And then when we did kick, we didn't have a good chase and so the ball was often down the throat of Foden without any pressure. That could wait for later though, when it was time to do the analysis. The simple fact was that we had beaten England at Twickenham. We had won the Triple Crown. It was a fantastic achievement.

We had talked about it beforehand. Some people don't consider the Triple Crown to be that big a deal these days. We do. It is in no way a diminished achievement to win it. Yes, winning the Championship and taking a Grand Slam were obviously the ultimate goals, but we wanted some silverware then and there as a reward for all our hard work. The Triple Crown was definitely a motivation for us all that week. Personally I hadn't won anything tangible playing for Wales, so this would be a great time and place to start.

It might have been an ugly performance, but to get the win under those circumstances shows how far we had come as a squad. As I said afterwards, 'Being away from home, it was brilliant to get the result. It will be carnage back home. We'll go back to Cardiff and we'll have an open-top bus planned for us probably!'

I thought the presentation of the Triple Crown would be an informal affair on the pitch. Then I was told I had to go all the way up those steps at Twickenham. When I eventually got to the top all I had eyes for was that Triple Crown. I almost walked past our chief executive Roger Lewis. I could hear someone screaming, 'Sam!' and thought it was a fan. 'Sorry, Roger,' I said when I realised my mistake, before shaking his hand and giving him a hug.

It was the best moment of my career to date. To lift the Triple Crown above my head at Twickenham surpassed anything else I had achieved. I was made man of the match too. What a day!

The players were going nuts. I think Ryan Jones's joy and excitement summed it up nicely. You couldn't have found a happier person. He had come on for Alun Wyn Jones in the second half and had certainly played his part. Ryan is one of the most passionate Welshmen I've ever met. He's been through some bad times, so he knows how to fully appreciate the good times. I think that's good for us youngsters in the team. Yes, some of us gently take the mick out of him. If we are doing a signing session with some young kids and he is nearby, I will tell the children, 'Go and call that bloke over there "Jug Head"!' And Dan and I are always calling him 'Dad', which I think annoys him. But it's only an expression of how much we admire him as a senior player. I think he's a brilliant captain; one of the best I've seen. He speaks so well to the team and he knows the game inside out. And if you want a cool head when the pressure is on, he is certainly your man. He always makes the right calls.

Twitter was going mad after the game. Ryan put on there: 'Eye spy with my little eye … something beginning with … TRIPLE CROWN!!' When we won the Grand Slam I'm not sure if he remembered doing that, so I sent him a message saying: '@RyanJonesOnline eye spy with my little eye something beginning with … GRAND SLAM!!'

Some of us got into a bit of trouble after the Triple Crown actually. In our excitement we posted some photos that we shouldn't have. I had one of me, Dan and Ryan with the Triple Crown which I tweeted, and I know Jamie Roberts and Jon Davies did something similar – they may have had their tops off too!

The Huw Evans Agency are our official photographers and they weren't happy. Media outlets were getting photos for free. The team management also made a very good point to us about how we don't like unauthorised people coming into the changing room. We consider it a sacred place. You have to earn the right to be in there, but here we were allowing the world in for free. It was wrong, and I can only apologise to Huw and everyone else. We learned our lesson. Twitter can be excellent, and it was marvellous to read all the messages of congratulation after this match, but we'd made a mistake there.

The match had turned on a moment of individual brilliance from Scott Williams. He'd come on at half-time to replace Jamie Roberts, who had hurt his knee.

I must tell you about Jamie before I tell you about Scott's try. He'd obviously hurt his knee quite badly. He was on crutches immediately, and was waving them around excitedly in all of the post-match photos. We thought that might be the last we saw of him for the campaign. But miraculously he was back training the following week. He played against both Italy and France, and was instantly christened 'Lazarus'. There was a great moment after we'd won the Grand Slam when everyone can be seen laughing and joking as a photo is taken of us with the Championship trophy. We were obviously ecstatic with our victory and the achievement of the Grand Slam, but the real reason everyone was laughing was because we were all chanting, 'Lazarus! Lazarus!' at Jamie!

In fairness, he has since had a serious knee operation, so he had clearly done some damage to himself. I don't think we ever doubted that, and we were hugely grateful for his courage and the performances he put in despite the injury. Alone of all the players he went home on the Saturday night after the match at Twickenham and stayed up all night icing his knee. But even the coaches were calling him 'Lazarus' . . .

Anyway, Scott had just missed a try-scoring opportunity when he had not seen Jon Davies and Leigh Halfpenny outside him. As Warren Gatland said afterwards, 'He should have passed, and if he had, it would have been a try. But he made amends by scoring himself later.'

He certainly did. It began when Courtney Lawes took the ball up the middle of the field, with less than five minutes of the match remaining. I was the man to tackle him first, taking him low. Ian Evans came in to help, as did Scott. We practise ripping the ball from an opponent a lot in training and Scott is very good at it. Scott wrestled the ball from Lawes and took off. He was now faced with about seven English defenders. So he kicked ahead. There was no one covering. Only Tom Croft had any chance of taking the ball.

I was still on the floor at this stage. I had looked up and seen Scott going through. I was just praying it would be a lucky bounce. It was. The ball bounced towards Scott and not Croft. Scott was over. I put my head in my hands, because I just couldn't believe it. It had been 12–12 before then. We had broken the deadlock. Leigh converted and it was 19–12.

England had been as tough as we'd expected them to be. They had stopped us from rumbling around the corner and they had competed really hard at the breakdown, where we thought Dan Cole – and Matt Stevens when he came on – were exceptional at the 'jackal'. Their midfield defence was rock solid, and Owen Farrell was very impressive too. He's a tough lad, that is for certain. He shocked one of our big forwards when he smashed into him, and gave him a few choice words afterwards too.

It was a punishing match, and I certainly felt it afterwards. I had a few stitches in my eye, an injury I think I sustained while making the last-gasp tackle on Manu Tuilagi. It was that sort of 'chop' tackle we practise regularly, but I just held on long enough so that he couldn't make the line. It felt like a normal tackle at the time, but now I realise it was rather more important than that.

England were leading 9–6. They had broken our line and I saw that we only had Alex Cuthbert defending on the blind-side. They had gone quite a long way past the gain line, so I ran in from an offside position to get back onside, as it were. I saw Tuilagi get the ball, and luckily it was going to be a side-on tackle which always makes it a bit easier. I was thinking, 'Close your eyes and dive at his ankles.' I suppose you've got to be willing to fly in head first and break your nose. I wanted to go as low as I could to get away from his fend. I did that and I hung on to him for my dear life. I didn't break my nose, but I did cut my eye open. Not that I noticed until after the game. I was washing my face at the sink in the changing rooms, and I saw a big gash under my eye, with some skin flapping out.

I'd never had stitches before, and I hate the thought of anything happening to my eyes or my teeth. Think of poor Gavin Quinnell, brother of Scott and Craig and son of Derek, who lost his sight in one eye after suffering an injury during Llanelli's Principality Premiership game against Cross Keys in 2010. That was horrific. So I tried to make out there was nothing wrong. But Rhys Williams, our consultant orthopaedic shoulder & knee surgeon, was in the changing room and noticed something was up. 'What's that?' he asked. He had a good look and gave me the news: 'That's going to need some stitches,' he said. He lay me down on the physio bed and I was sweating profusely. It was not a good experience, as he put in five or six stitches. I could feel my eyelid pulling, and there was pressure on my eyeball.

It was even worse when they were taken out by Professor

John Williams a week later. Then it felt like my eyelid was going to come off completely. I was sweating even more then! To think of all the injuries I've had, and this one was causing me the most grief.

Leigh's heroics, Scott's try, even my tackle. They were all important. But so was the ten-minute period in the second half when Rhys Priestland was sin-binned for tackling Alex Corbisiero from an off-side position. The way we reacted then was superb. Farrell kicked the resultant penalty to make it 12–6 to England, but they did not score again during that period – or during the match as it happened. And we even got a penalty of our own, kicked by Leigh, during that sin-bin period.

We were under the posts after Rhys was sin-binned, and everyone just sort of looked at each other. Everyone was thinking the same thing. This was crunch time. We couldn't let our heads drop. We'd lost Six Nations matches before when people had been sin-binned. Indeed, we'd lost one in 2010 when Alun Wyn Jones was yellow-carded. But we weren't going to lose this one because we were down to fourteen men.

We just had to keep the ball. The ball was kicked to Leigh, and once a ruck was set up around the halfway line, we just kept it by picking-and-going. It may not have been pretty but it certainly ran down the clock. We kept the ball for nearly five uninterrupted minutes. I think we went through nearly nineteen phases. In all I think we had it for nearly eight and a half minutes of the ten for which Rhys was in the sin-bin.

During this period I thought of the England 2003 World

Cup winner, hooker Steve Thompson. Were you watching you may have noticed that there was a curious moment during that five-minute period of 'keep ball' when I appeared to be signalling for help as I ran with the ball. I was worried about being isolated in the middle of the field against some big English forwards. So first I signalled for some forwards to help, and then, when that didn't happen, I just ran back towards them. I learned that from Thompson. I'd seen him do that – and be praised by the commentators – all those years ago.

There was an incident during the second half that I feel I need to clear up, as I'm not sure the words I uttered afterwards came out quite as I might have liked. It was the incident at a line-out when I was lifted high in the air, and England's captain Chris Robshaw touched me as I was in the air and I went crashing to the floor. We received a penalty, but no card was issued. Robshaw had nudged my feet and my whole body had tilted sideways. It looked as if my lifters hadn't done their job properly, but the truth is that it is almost impossible to keep hold once the player you are lifting goes sideways.

It was an accident. And it produced a brilliant action photo, which I've still got on my iPhone. But it was a long way down, and the landing certainly hurt. I did think momentarily of Vincent Clerc and how I thought he had milked my tackle on him in that World Cup semi-final.

But what I worded wrongly was what my teammates said. I didn't mean to say they were encouraging me to milk it. They wouldn't do that. They might have been saying that I should have taken my time in getting up, and maybe received some attention from the physio because it was a nasty fall, but they would not have tried to con the referee.

I was quoted as saying, 'I was not going to play the hypocrite or act like a footballer.' That's because I always criticise footballers for staying down. As I mentioned earlier, I never want to show that I am hurt, and that's why I try to get up straight away whenever I can.

I was chuffed that in the tunnel afterwards Chris asked to swap shirts. I thought he had had an excellent game. People say he is not a specialist seven, but he hurt us at the breakdown and he seemed to be everywhere on the pitch. He epitomised the effort England put in.

It was a nice moment because I never ask my opponent to swap shirts. I just wouldn't want them to say no! I've played against the likes of George Smith, Richie McCaw, Heinrich Brussow, Thierry Dusautoir and David Pocock, and I haven't got any of their jerseys. I might regret that one day, but I just haven't felt able to ask them. I have got Sean O'Brien's jersey from the World Cup quarter-final against Ireland, and was really pleased that he asked. The only player I have ever asked was on my side: Martyn Williams, when we played New Zealand in 2010. I started, and he was on the bench. I knew he wouldn't say no because he is a mate. And a hero!

Talking of which, I met Jason Leonard at the after-match function. He is someone I've looked up to since I was kid, so it was marvellous to meet him. I spent about fifteen minutes talking to him. He really is a top bloke.

I was late for that function because I was doing some press

duties. Apparently Ryan had done all the formalities by the time I got there, but I didn't want to appear rude, so I went up, apologised and said a few words. After that I was so tired that I just sat at the table day-dreaming. The players kept catching me doing it, and were taking the mick out of me. I just said: 'I'm spent!'

It had been so hectic after the game. Not least because we all had to do three and a half minutes of cryotherapy in the mobile chambers which were situated across the car park on the west side of the ground. The van pulling it could not get closer to the changing rooms. So that was interesting, making our way through the crowds. Loads of people were asking for autographs, but you couldn't stop on the way there. If you'd have stopped for one, you would have been there for an hour. So we said, 'If you wait until afterwards, we will do them then.' And some did wait, and we did sign for them before heading back to the changing rooms.

I also had a bang on the knee, so along with others like Alun Wyn Jones and Rhys Priestland, I had to stay at the team hotel that night icing my injury. Some of the boys went out, but there was nothing silly.

I couldn't find any chocolate anywhere (although in an interview on the Sunday, BBC Wales gave me some, including my favourite Fruit & Nut bar), so I just had some chips and chicken wings!

The following Wednesday I was back in London. This time I was at 10 Downing Street for a special St David's Day reception on

the eve of the day itself. I went with Warren Gatland, Alan
Phillips, Roger Lewis and David Pickering (WRU chairman).
And there were all sorts of big names from Welsh life there. I
didn't realise until later that Joanna Page from *Gavin & Stacey*
was there. I love that programme. So does David Cameron, the
Prime Minister, apparently, according to his speech that day.

It was a very good speech, in which I was honoured that he
mentioned me. On his way in he had spoken to a few people
and one of them had been me, and he clearly knew his rugby.
He knew who we'd played and whom we had left to play. We
had a decent chat.

This was his speech in full:

A very warm welcome to you all. It's great to have you here.
I think it's been an incredible few years for Wales.
Obviously it's the Dickens anniversary this year, so I was
going to describe it as 'the best of times, the worst of times'.
Clearly, the best of times in that there's no doubt in my
mind that Wales has produced the finest sitcom to come out
in the last five years: of course, Gavin & Stacey. I think we
have some of the cast here tonight, have we? Very good.
Well, it's tidy to have you here. I'm a huge fan. Like all sit-
coms in the United Kingdom, it was much too short. We
needed more episodes, but an absolutely fantastic piece of
work and it gave pleasure to absolutely millions. So that was
the best of times.

Obviously, of course, the best of times with – and it hurts
me to say this, as an England rugby fan. I know Sam is here.

It was an absolutely magnificent performance, and it was actually great to see two such young teams playing so well. Obviously when the crunch comes in the future, I will always be on the white side rather than the red side, but it was great to see you play so well with such heart and with such strength in that last game. So, many congratulations to the Welsh rugby team.

But obviously alongside the best of times, there was the worst of times. That great performance in the Rugby World Cup, but obviously a very sad game against the French. I feel some sympathy. I have had a bit of a run in with the French recently, so I know what you went through, but it was tremendous.

A Welsh choir sang too – children from the London Welsh School – and afterwards Warren and I went in to see them. They clearly weren't expecting us, but when they did see us the reception they gave us was stunning. They started screaming and shouting. We gladly signed autographs and pictures, and chatted to them all.

This was one of the perks of being captain of Wales. Another was when I was asked to carry the Olympic Torch in Cardiff on 25 May 2012. What an experience that was. I described it as a 'great moment in my life', and it was. The crowds that turned out were fantastic, and it was fitting that I ran past the Millennium Stadium with the torch.

Looking back, I would have been gutted to have missed out on opportunities like these. I'm so glad that I didn't turn the captaincy down. I probably knew at the time that this would be the case, but I was reluctant to leap out of my comfort zone. I can only thank those who persuaded me to do it.

Being 'Captain Cymru' wasn't so bad after all.

11

Italian Job

I'd done more than bang my knee. I knew exactly what I'd done. I'd damaged my medial collateral ligament. It had been in the early stages of the match against England at Twickenham. I had taken a ball off Rhys Priestland in the middle of the field and driven at the English defence. I was tackled from the side by the England lock Geoff Parling and felt a tweak in my left knee as it was pushed inwards.

I'd suffered a similar injury in Paris in the 2011 Six Nations, and had been replaced after just fifteen minutes. This time it didn't feel quite as serious, so I was desperate to stay on. But I knew that I'd damaged my MCL.

I'm not claiming to be a medical expert, but when you've played a certain amount of sport and suffered a few injuries, you get to know these things. You've got more than a good idea what you've done, and how serious it is.

Mark Davies, the physio, came on. 'I don't mean to sound as if I know it all, but I've definitely done something to my MCL,' I said. He quickly did all the tests to confirm that it was indeed an injury to my MCL. Thankfully he also confirmed that it had not been ruptured. So, under the posts while England kicked a penalty, he strapped it up. It was strapped even more tightly at half-time.

There was no way I was going off. I'd gone off against Ireland, I'd missed Scotland – I wasn't going off again, even if for the rest of the match I got shooting pains in my knee every few minutes. When I watched the game back afterwards, there was one moment when I came out of a ruck and then went straight to the ground, doubled in pain, and then got up and carried on. I think people thought that it was a recurrence of the dead leg that had forced me off in the first match of the campaign against Ireland and that meant I had missed the match against Scotland. It was the same leg after all, and there was already a considerable amount of strapping protecting it.

I saw our knee surgeon, Rhys Williams, immediately after the game and he confirmed that it was a grade 1 medial collateral ligament sprain, as opposed to the grade 2 injury I'd suffered in France. I asked what the timescale for recovery was, and was told that it depended on how my rehabilitation went.

I could walk without a limp. That was a good thing, but it also had its downside, as some people naturally assumed that I was fit, or at least was not far off being fit. That was not the case. So I did get a little cheesed off because I had the feeling that I was being questioned. I remember getting home after the England game and watching the TV, which showed a clip of me coming off the team bus at the Vale Hotel. The point was being made that I looked fit enough, and it was being assumed that I would be fine for the Italy game in a fortnight. If only it were that simple. I could do things in a straight line, whether it was walking or even jogging, but as soon as I tried to do anything laterally or particularly explosively, I was in trouble.

The truth was that I was struggling to make even the France game. That's how bad the knee was, and how long the recovery might be. That anyone might think that I was bottling it really annoyed me. I was determined to do everything in my power to make sure that I had a chance for the Italy match. As I said earlier, I never want to miss a Test match. I began icing my knee the night after the England match, and, using the special 'Game Ready' ice-machine, continued to do so day and night thereafter.

But by the Friday after the England game, with eight days to go until the Italy match, I knew that I was struggling. I always try to be positive in these situations, and if I'm not, Andy McCann will make sure I am. But this was not looking good. I saw Prav Mathema, and even he admitted that I was in trouble. I said to him, 'What can I do to give myself a chance, even if it is only the smallest chance?' He said that I could only keep on doing the icing religiously, and then also suggested some exercises that might help my range of movement in the knee.

Right, that was it. I was going to go home that weekend, and I was going to work harder than I'd ever worked before on any injury. I was going to turn up at the Vale Hotel on Monday morning and shock Prav. I was going to make sure he said something like, 'I can't believe it, Sam. There is such an improvement. You might be able to play against Italy after all.' That was my aim.

And that's what I did. I worked so hard that weekend. If some people thought that I was merely rested for the Italy match, and that it did not matter to me that I missed it, they should have seen me that weekend. I could not have been more dedicated or determined. I worked my socks off.

I turned up on Monday morning, and as usual we all went in straight away for our medical screenings. Prav was expecting to have a quick look at me and rule me out of the match. But he couldn't. I'd achieved my aim. I'd shocked him.

'I reckon I can play,' I said, as I demonstrated to him that I could squat almost fully. I'd gone from limited movement to almost full range of movement in a few days.

'You've made real progress, Sam,' he said. He couldn't rule me out yet. The team was being announced the following day; he was going to have to push me further and see how I reacted.

I was actually quite proud that I'd got that far. It was a small success in my ever-continuing battle never to accept defeat. I'd shown that a positive attitude and loads of hard work could overcome certain hurdles.

So Prav went through some exercises that pushed me further and further in my rehabilitation. Then he asked me to do a dynamic step off my left leg. I felt a sharp pain immediately

242

and let out a yelp. I looked at Prav and he just gave me the slit-throat sign that I knew meant that I was out of the Italy game.

Talking to Warren much later he said that they were actually quite glad because they wanted to give Justin Tipuric a game. They would obviously have wanted him to play against Scotland, but, like me, he had been injured, and they said that they wanted to give him at least one start in the campaign.

But that did not mean that I wasn't massively disappointed to miss out. My head was gone. My dad had been on the phone again asking how fit I was, but this time I did not get close. I had to relay the bad news on the Monday, that when the team was announced on the Tuesday he should not expect my name to be in it. I knew how disappointed he would be.

I now had to focus on the France match the week after. I was asking all the physios what my chances were, but they were not giving too much away. You couldn't blame them. They just kept saying that I needed to be running properly before any real assessment could be made.

It was always going to be touch and go, but I was leaving nothing to chance. I had to be a little bit selfish, if I was honest. I had to stay off my leg as much as possible. That's why I pulled out of some commercial and charity appearances in that week before Italy. I know that may have disappointed some people, but if that extra bit of rest and treatment paid off, then I was sure that I would be forgiven.

It was time to hit the swimming pool in my bid to get fit. I did some savage sessions in the pool up at the Vale Hotel with the conditioner John Ashby. Most of the time I was only allowed to use my upper body so he would tie my feet together. And he would also make me swim underwater a lot to try to develop as much lactic acid as I could. It was so hard.

I can only apologise to a group of schoolchildren who were in there one day for the state I was in as John pushed me to the limit. I was swimming a series of lengths as fast as I could, and with little rest in between, and some of the noises I was making as I gasped for air on the edge of the pool were not good. I'm not a bad swimmer usually, but this was seriously testing me and I was grunting and groaning.

I'd been captain in twelve Tests by this stage, with only three at the Millennium Stadium (the Barbarians, England in the World Cup warm-up, and Australia in December). So I still hadn't captained Wales in a Six Nations match at the Millennium Stadium.

Gethin Jenkins was made captain for the match, even though Matthew Rees had returned to the side in place of Ken Owens to ensure that the 2009 British and Irish Lions front row of him, Gethin and Adam Jones was together for the first time in this Championship, and for only the fourth time since that Lions tour. Of that decision to choose Gethin ahead of Matthew, Warren said: 'We've got guys with different leadership styles. Sam leads by example on the pitch, while Matthew leads from the front. He is an intelligent forward. They all have different strengths . . . Rhys Priestland calls a lot of the shots behind, while Jamie Roberts and Dan Lydiate also have responsible roles. There are players taking responsibility everywhere.'

And Warren was right. There were leaders everywhere. It was one reason why I felt so much more comfortable in the role now. I didn't walk around the team hotel worrying that people were looking at me and judging me. I used to think they were thinking: 'He shouldn't be Wales captain.' I'd be worrying about which meetings I had to speak at. Now I'd almost forgotten that I was captain. I was just cracking on.

Justin was replacing me at openside, of course, and 'Lazarus' had risen from the dead to take his place at centre, with Scott Williams dropping back to the bench after his Twickenham heroics. Also on the bench was Luke Charteris, who was featuring for the first time in the Six Nations after recovering from his wrist injury, and James Hook, who had had chicken pox and had withdrawn from the replacements bench at Twickenham to be replaced by Stephen Jones.

All joking aside about Jamie Roberts, it was interesting to hear him say in an interview that he was very nervous about his selection for this Italy match. He had been the Lions player of the series not that long before and had been one of our best players at the World Cup. If he was nervous, then we all had reason to be. It was a solid indication that we possessed serious strength in depth. There were some positions that people thought were weak in cover, but I never thought that. Take scrum-half, where Mike Phillips was playing out of his skin, but where I think Lloyd Williams is an amazing prospect. He's a very different player from Mike, but I think he will be a top player. And players like Luke being on the bench meant we had a lot of experience coming back into the squad at a good time. Usually you are losing loads of players at such a stage of a campaign, but we seemed to be gaining them, with Matthew and Luke coming back for this game.

I certainly knew Justin was pushing me. By no means did I think my place was certain. Nobody was, or is, safe in this Wales side. I knew how good Justin was. He'd shown that in the second half against Ireland. He is a classy player with nice hands and he is a really good scrapper on the floor. And I thought he would fit into this Wales side easily, because with the low tacklers like Gethin and Dan Lydiate, it would allow Justin to go in on the ball. He's also a good line-out forward, so he ticks all the boxes.

He's a genuine openside flanker these days, but not many people know that we played in the same Wales Under-20s side at the 2008 IRB Junior World Championship played in Wales. Before the Italy game I was looking through some old photos with Toby Faletau and he was mocking my terrible hair cut when he spotted Justin in the same photo. 'I didn't realise you played with Justin,' he said.

Neither of us was playing in our favoured number seven shirt back then. And neither was Josh Turnbull, the Scarlets openside whose 2011/12 season was unfortunately plagued by injury. Josh was at lock, I was at No. 8 and Justin was at blind-side flanker. Playing elsewhere probably had its benefits for me, Josh and Justin. Nowadays the openside has to be destructive in his play, and our physicality probably improved as we had to carry so much in our other positions.

The openside in that U20 team? A lad from Cardiff called

Dan Franks, who sadly had to give up the game through injury. When we were in the Cardiff Blues Academy together, Dan was assigned to play for the Cardiff RFC semi-professional side, while I went to Glamorgan Wanderers. No disrespect to the Wanderers – I loved my time there – but I can only presume that the Blues thought Dan was the better prospect. And as I write I hear that Dan is contemplating a comeback. That is great news. I hope he succeeds in it.

I'd had a good look at Italy. Justin and I had been asked by the management to do some analysis on them in attack and defence, and present it to the team on the Thursday before the match. It was the first time I'd done that. If I'm honest, it was not a complicated analysis. Italy do not do complicated when it comes to Test-match rugby. They rely on their heavy forwards, and No. 8 Sergio Parisse and flanker Alessandro Zanni are key players for them. Parisse quite rightly receives a lot of plaudits, but Zanni is a little underestimated, I reckon. His work at the breakdown, in carrying and tackling, is unbelievable.

Before the team was announced I said to the press: 'We must be ruthless. This is a great opportunity to send a message out to France that we are not messing around. We want a good, impressive performance against the Italians to try and get some negative thoughts into the French minds before they come to Cardiff.'

I knew that it would not be easy: 'When you watch a game, like say ours against Scotland, it can look as though it is a comfortable eighty minutes,' I said. 'But when you play in it, you know what a hard struggle it is to get a victory like that. You have to work so hard for it. That has always been the case when I've played Italy. Even though some of our wins against them might have looked comfortable from a spectators' point of view, none have ever come easily. The boys who have played them before know what to expect. You have to break them down and if you are complacent and allow them to get their tails up with thirty minutes to go, then you are in trouble.

'They beat France last year, albeit at home, and so they have that level of performance in them. I can understand some people getting ahead of themselves and looking past Italy to the France game. But the players know better than to do that, and that's why we will really knuckle down in training this week. It was great to get that first win against Ireland because since then everyone has been really positive and confident. That makes a massive difference to training because it makes you push yourself harder because you want to succeed even more. It has definitely been the best campaign I've been part of. That atmosphere is just top class.'

And it was. I again declined the offer from the team management to sit on the bench with the replacements and some of the staff. I just wanted to be treated like any other player. That is how everyone is in the squad. There are no egos that run out of control. Instead I watched the match from the president's box with Lloyd Williams, who had a thigh strain and had been replaced on the bench by Rhys Webb.

We were sitting there before kick-off in our suits, when I realised that shots of the ground were being shown on the big screen. It always makes me laugh when people in the crowd are shown on the screen. They always want to make a funny face or wave at the camera, but they often can't do so properly because they cannot find where the camera is quickly enough before it moves on.

So I had a little plan. I was going to embarrass Lloyd. I scanned the ground for the camera that was likely to be used to show a shot of us. And sure enough it to came to us as we sat there waiting for the game to start. As it did, I grabbed Lloyd's arm and threw it up in the air as if we were celebrating together. He tried to put his arm down, but I wouldn't let go as I went nuts with the camera on me and him. I'm not sure the committee behind us in the box knew what to make of it. The Wales captain was on something. Or he was just having a laugh with one of his mates.

At least the president's box was a little quieter than the box Matthew Rees and I had sat in for the Scotland game. Then we'd been signing things non-stop, but here we could relax.

I'd felt a bit strange in the changing room when I'd spent some time in there before the game. I'd had one of those moments when you realise how much you enjoy playing for Wales. I was sitting in a corner on my own when Rob Howley came over and said, 'It's horrible not playing, isn't it?'

Sometimes when you're playing and feeling under pressure, you wonder why you do it, and why you put yourself through such worry. You wish you were the bloke standing there injured so that you don't have to go through it. Then when you are that bloke standing there not able to play you realise how much you want to play, how much you want to run out into the stadium that day.

We beat Italy 24–3, but it was a frustrating afternoon. We made an awful lot of handling errors and were penalised a lot at the breakdown, especially in attack. To say the breakdown was a mess was an understatement. There were twenty-five penalties given in the match overall, and at least fifteen of them came at the breakdown, and most of them were given to the defending team.

We knew beforehand that the Italians were going to be lying on the wrong side and competing hard at the breakdown. We also knew that referee George Clancy was quite strict on players coming in from the side at that area, and in that respect it was probably a difficult game to referee, because it was so scrappy and there was so much going on at the contact area.

That is not to say that I thought Justin had a bad game. Far from it. He had an outstanding match. His linking skills in particular were superb. He should have been man of the match in my view. That award went to wing Alex Cuthbert, but I was interested to see when I got home and watched the match on TV that Jonathan Davies (the BBC pundit, not our current centre) was going to give it to Justin and then decided late on to give it to Alex. That's what scoring a try three minutes from time does for you!

It was an excellent try though, as Gethin took a quick penalty on halfway and found Alex, who targeted the replacement prop Fabio Staibano in the defensive line and skinned him. He was also too quick for the covering Giulio Toniolatti at the corner.

Disappointingly, that was only our second try of the match. We had so much possession, but both of our tries only came in the second half after we had been 9–3 up at half-time through three Leigh Halfpenny penalties.

Jamie Roberts scored that first try, and a fine solo effort it was that began with Alun Wyn Jones snaffling a loose ball well inside our own half. The ball was moved left quickly through Justin, Phillsy, Leigh and then Rhys Priestland. Jamie took a lovely angle off Rhys on halfway and, with the Italian defence all at sea because they had been attacking, ran all the way to score. I think he'd proved that he warranted a place. And a bit more.

We might have scored again when Ryan Jones went over after Jamie had gone through a gap, but there was a little bit of blocking from Rhys Webb, who had come on to make his Test debut. I thought he did really well in the last ten minutes for which he was on; another sign of our depth.

We'd also had other chances that were close to producing tries. Leigh was twice denied by excellent tackles from Parisse, Alex might have scored previously after a long pass from Jon Davies, who had an outstanding game, and Justin also went close.

We had so much possession that we did not have to make that many tackles. But when we did, we did not miss any, I don't think. Shaun Edwards said afterwards that he thought it had been like a training session in that regard, because we had been so accurate with our tackling. He clearly did not think anyone had done enough tackling, however, because the following Tuesday he gave us a massively hard defensive session to make sure we were up to speed for the France game.

Leigh was desperately unlucky to receive a yellow card in the second half. First of all play should not have been going on because a blatant knock on by Mirco Bergamasco was missed. Then Leigh chased his own high kick and had his eyes on the ball all the time as he challenged Parisse in the air. It didn't look great, but there was no way it was a deliberate foul. Thankfully it didn't matter too much. We did not concede a point during that period. But I think Leigh might have very rightfully contested a £30,000 fine for that one!

The boys were disappointed afterwards. In the changing rooms you would not have thought that we had won. I'm not sure that Gethin and Rhys Priestland, who are in charge of the after-match music, knew what to put on. They would normally put on the 'happy' music after a win, but this was a little awkward.

I quite liked it, though. Here we were, having won 24–3, and we were disappointed. That showed how far we had come as a team.

There had just been too many handling errors. I think there were ten in total. The set piece was very good, with the scrummage a 100 per cent success and with thirteen of the fourteen line-outs won.

'The boys are a bit flat in the dressing room,' said Warren. 'I thought they really wanted to score some points today and didn't really get a chance. I thought we played some great rugby in the first half. The man with the whistle didn't make it easy for us, I thought he was pedantic. That was a little bit frustrating. But the boys tried really hard and at the end of the day we're four from four.'

The Grand Slam was on. Only France stood in our way.

12

The Slam

It was a terrible shock to hear the news the morning before the France match. The great Mervyn Davies had passed away.

I had never met 'Merv the Swerve', as he was known to almost everyone in rugby, but by coincidence Andy McCann had given me his book, *In Strength and Shadow*, a couple of weeks before. He had thought it would be of interest. Sadly I never got around to reading it. I wish I had. And I wish I'd met Merv.

His death at the age of sixty-five made an already emotional occasion even more emotional. As players we were all aware of what a great player he had been: that he had led Wales to the Grand Slam in 1976 and that he had played his part in the 1971 and 1974 British Lions' sides in New Zealand and South

Africa. We also knew that his career had been tragically cut short three weeks after that 1976 Grand Slam when he suffered a brain haemorrhage playing for Swansea against Pontypool in a Welsh Cup semi-final.

Now his life had been cut short too. It was only natural and right that we wore black armbands for the match, and that we observed a minute's silence for Merv, and for New Zealand's Jock Hobbs, who had also died in the same week.

It also made us more determined to win the Grand Slam. I wanted to be a Grand Slam-winning captain just like 'Merv the Swerve'. As I wrote in my *Daily Telegraph* column on the morning of the game: 'We're confident. We feel we deserve the Grand Slam after all the effort we've put in. We feel it would be our just reward. And, should we win, I would be hugely privileged to stand alongside Mervyn Davies in the illustrious list of Wales' Grand Slam captains.'

And yes, I was fit. I had begun doing some running on the morning of the Italy match up at the Vale Hotel, while some of the players were doing their 'physical primers'. By 'physical primers' I mean they were doing some explosive movement work in order to stimulate their nervous systems. This is a rel-atively new addition to some players' match preparation, and something that not many teams do, so I gather. And I must admit that it is not something I do. I prefer to chill out in my room, as does Toby Faletau. You'd never catch him doing a 'physical primer' on the morning of a match. But George North swears by them, as do most of the back-three players. At mid-morning they will do exercises like plyometric jumps,

10-metre sprints and heavy shot putts to arouse their nervous systems.

By Tuesday I was almost training fully, which was good news, not least because I could no longer be referred to as 'Team-run Warby' amongst the boys. Of course, it was bad news for Justin Tipuric, who had played so well against Italy. He wasn't even on the replacements bench.

I was the only change in the starting line-up from the Italy match, with Lloyd Williams coming back onto the replacements bench instead of Rhys Webb as the only change there.

I was really happy with the way the knee had responded. On the Tuesday I had done 90 per cent of the session. And as I mentioned, it was a hard defensive session organised by Shaun Edwards. He was making sure that everybody made up for the lack of tackles in the Italy match.

But while that was a good session, the session on the Thursday began as a shocker. It was our last proper session before the match, but it was going horribly wrong for some reason. Balls were being dropped all over the place. As captain I was thinking: 'I'm going to have stop this session and have a chat with the boys here.' It was that bad.

Just as I was thinking that, Adam Jones decided he'd seen enough. This was another example of the importance of the senior players within a squad, and especially within our squad. There has been so much talk about the youngsters in this Wales squad that I think, amidst all this praise, the influence of the senior players has been understated and undervalued. Adam shouted for everyone to come in, and he was very blunt in his assessment. 'Calm down,' he said to everyone. There might have been the odd swear word in there too. 'We do this session every Thursday before a Test and we do it well,' he said. 'The game is still forty-eight hours away. Let's all relax.'

He was right. Everybody was too uptight and trying too hard. But after that the session went OK. The voice of experience had spoken.

Maybe the fifteen minutes or so at the start of that session were an indication of what a mad week it was. A Grand Slam week can't really be anything else, but this was obviously even madder because it was the first time we had played France since that semi-final in Auckland. And I, as the man who had been sent off in that match, was clearly going to be in the spotlight.

I knew it would be a topic of discussion at the pre-match press conference. It had to be. And sure enough one of the French journalists was very quick to ask me about the absence of my friend Vincent Clerc with a shoulder injury from the France team sheet.

'It makes no difference to me at all,' I said. 'There are much more important things to worry about this weekend and my knee has distracted me from it, to be honest. I have just wanted to get that right over the last three weeks. This week I've just been trying to make sure the team and myself are ready for the game at the weekend. That hasn't crept into my mind.' I also mentioned that I was rather keen to last more than twenty minutes against the French, having been injured after just fifteen minutes in the 2011 Six Nations fixture in Paris, and then, of course, not lasting too long in the semi-final. In the 2010 home fixture when we'd lost 26–20 I had been on the bench but had not been used.

'I have played France twice now and haven't made it past the twenty-minute mark on both occasions,' I said. 'The first time I got injured, and then there was obviously the World Cup semi-final, so it would be nice just to stay on the field a bit longer this time. But I would also like a good outing against Thierry Dusautoir, the world player of the year and someone I respect very highly.'

I have a confession to make here. I couldn't say as much at the time, because it would have fuelled things unnecessarily ahead of the match, but I was very conscious of the World Cup semi-final that week. Yes, I was playing it down in public, but in private I was actually watching the tape of the *That Semi Final* TV programme. When I had first watched it, it had made me very emotional. Now I wanted it to make me angry. Yes, it would doubtless make me emotional too, but I wanted it to get my adrenalin pumping, to fire me up even more for the Grand Slam match.

I'd kept the programme on my TV as a reminder. Now, whenever I got a quiet moment at home, I would switch it on. And it did make me angry. It made me more determined to win the Grand Slam. It also worried me that my emotions might get the better of me during the national anthems. That scene where everyone fell silent in the stadium while watching the match so many thousands of miles away, was difficult to erase from my mind. If I thought about it during the anthems there was a good chance that my bottom lip would be going.

And that's exactly what happened. I did think about that moment during the anthems. I thought about all those people who had been standing where I was now standing. I thought about how, in a couple of hours time, things could be very different. And my bottom lip did start going. But I just about managed to hold it together.

This was no ordinary match. I began to realise that on my day off on the Wednesday, when I went for my weekly supermarket shop. The number of people coming up to me to talk about the game and wish the team good luck was very different from usual. There was some buzz – and that was on the Wednesday!

We had nine players who had been involved in the Grand Slam of 2008 (and indeed three – Gethin Jenkins, Adam Jones and Ryan Jones – who had been involved in the Grand Slam of 2005), and they had told the rest of us what to expect. Cardiff would be 'absolutely mental', they reckoned. There was certainly going to be no problem in the players getting through their full quota of ten tickets for this match. They were like gold dust. Sometimes for home games you might be able to get fifteen or twenty tickets each (with four of them free and the others having to be paid for). There was no chance of that for this game. It was a strict ten each.

Another confession. Sorting tickets before a match stresses me. It always has. I was talking to my dad about this and he said he had been reading Roy Keane's book and that Keane had said that he once walked out for an FA Cup Final worrying about tickets. That actually made me feel better. It wasn't just me.

It's not that I'm complaining about my friends and family

wanting to come and watch me play for Wales. Of course I'm not. I'm as proud of them as they are of me, and I want to help as many of them as I can, but sometimes it is not just possible. Rachel always goes with the other players' wives and girlfriends, so there are four free tickets for my mum and dad, Ben and Holly. Then Holly's husband Chris always comes, as do Rachel's parents, Geoff and Sue, and sometimes Rachel's sisters Sarah and Kate. My dad sensed I was really stressing before the France match. So he just said to me: 'Give me the ten tickets, tell me who needs them and I will sort it out.' It was a weight off my mind.

This was the biggest match of my life. I considered it a bigger match than the World Cup semi-final, because we had the opportunity to win something so prestigious rather than reach a final. It was obvious that there would be the most extraordinary atmosphere I'd ever encountered in any match. I mentioned earlier the noise in 2010 when Shane Williams scored that last-gasp try to beat Scotland, and that I couldn't hear what the player next to me was saying. I fully expected it to be like that for most of the game – and it was.

I remember watching the Grand Slams in 2005 and 2008 and they were a big part of what made me want to play rugby. You see those moments and they are something you want to be a part of. I was sitting at home watching the 2008 Grand Slam match on TV with my dad and brother, when about three minutes from time, my hero Martyn Williams picked up from a ruck and sniped over to score. The Millennium Stadium crowd went ballistic and Martyn was mobbed by his teammates. I can remember thinking to myself: 'What an amazing feeling that must be.' And four years later, here I was with the chance of finding out how amazing that feeling might be.

We were being compared to the great Wales team of the 1970s, who won three Grand Slams between 1971 and 1978. But I wasn't getting drawn into that comparison. 'It is difficult to compare,' I said. 'I was fortunate enough to meet JPR (Williams) the other day and he told me he beat England eleven consecutive times at senior level. So until we do that I don't think we can compete!'

At last I was getting to captain Wales at the Millennium Stadium in a Six Nations match, but I wasn't going to be leading the team out. It was to be Matthew Rees's fiftieth cap for Wales, so it was him rather than me going out first, just as Ian Gough did for his fiftieth cap instead of captain Ryan Jones in the 2008 Grand Slam match.

Matthew thoroughly deserved the honour. He has been a wonderful player and ambassador for his country, and I was very mindful of the fact that I would not have been captain in the first place had he not suffered an injury in the previous summer and missed the World Cup.

Oddly it meant that I still hadn't led Wales out at home wearing the red jersey. When I skippered against the Barbarians in my first match in charge and against Australia immediately after the World Cup, they were the occasions of Stephen Jones's 100th cap and Shane Williams's farewell from international rugby. It was only right and proper that those two players led out the team. And then when we had played, and beaten, England at home in the summer World Cup match, we had worn our change strip of black (just as England had worn black at home against us the previous week).

I have never seen the breakfast room so quiet and serious as it was that morning before the France match. It just meant so much. As is usual, I was sharing a room with Dan Lydiate, and we just tried to chill, but it wasn't easy. This really was the calm before the storm, as we lay on our beds listening to our music. I was so nervous. Waiting for kick-off is always hard, but this seemed harder.

The Vale Hotel was heaving. There were fans and autograph hunters everywhere. There are always quite a few there, but this was on a different scale. So, unusually, parts of the hotel were sectioned off. If we didn't want to speak to anyone, we didn't have to. People who haven't played sport to the highest level might not be able to understand that, but it is not being rude. It is just that 'game faces' are not a cliché. You need the space to get them right.

I didn't once go near the main hotel foyer. I know that upset some fans, because a mate of mine, Rhys Dyer, who plays scrum-half for Cross Keys, was there with his son Alfie, and he told me afterwards that he had to explain to a few of them why I had done it. 'You can't expect them to sign autographs and chat with fans just before the Grand Slam match,' he told them.

Just before we left for the stadium we had our usual team meeting, in which Warren and Rob Howley spoke for five or ten minutes. I made sure I took my boots with me to that meeting.

On the day before the game we go to the stadium to do the team run, and we take our suits and boots with us to leave there in readiness for the next day. Sometimes, though, you might want to take your boots back to the hotel to do a line-out session on the morning of the match. If you risk that without leaving a spare pair at the ground, you've got to be aware amidst all the nerves and tension the next day to remember your boots. I'd done that. I was OK.

We had the meeting and straightaway went through the crowd to board the bus. Not a word was said. The police escort was ready in front of us. Everyone had their headphones on. This was it.

Alan Phillips was one of the last to get on the bus. He stood at the front and made himself heard. 'Whose boots are these then?' he asked.

Oh no. In some embarrassment I raised my hand apologetically. I'd left my boots in the team room. I could have gone to the Grand Slam match without any boots. I did say that I could be forgetful. Thumper had saved me. He knows to watch out for me now.

After the Grand Slam match, he, Jamie Roberts and I had to go to Paris to see WRU sponsors Eden Park in order to choose some new suits for the team. The night before we left I picked up an answerphone message on my mobile. It was Thumper. 'Sam, I know what you're like,' he said. He then shouted the word 'PASSPORT' five times. 'Put it in your bag now!' and he hung up. I remembered my passport.

I shall never forget the bus journey to the stadium that day on Saturday 17 March 2012. It is always a special journey, but this was extra special. We go from our Vale Hotel base along the M4 for one junction, then off down the A4232 for a few miles before turning off at Leckwith, passing the Cardiff City Stadium, then along Cowbridge Road East and over the River Taff, before turning right into Westgate Street alongside the famous old Angel Hotel and our home again now at the Cardiff Blues, the Arms Park. The bus is clearly distinguishable as the team bus, with a 'Wales Team' sign at the front and the number plate BU55 WRU. Even on the M4 cars were hooting their horns at us. That was unusual.

Along the way we were shown a three-minute video clip of all the tries we'd scored in the previous twelve months. It was very powerful stuff and a reminder of how well we had played in that time.

By the time we turned right into Westgate Street it was absolutely crazy. I had never seen Cardiff so chock-a-block. All the players had taken off their headphones so they could hear the noise outside. It was unbelievable. I don't think I was the only one who took a photo on my iPhone as a memento of the remarkable scenes. Even after we won, it remained one of the best parts of the day. It reminded us all how lucky we were to be playing a Grand Slam game at home in front of our own fans. It was a journey that you just wanted to last for hours. It was awesome; truly inspirational.

So to the game itself. It wasn't pretty, but it was never going to be. France had asked that the stadium roof stay open, thereby announcing their intentions early. There was a lot of kicking, that was for sure. Their fly-half Lionel Beauxis likes doing that and we knew what was coming.

It can be frustrating when people do not understand the rationale of the kicking battle. It is so easy to criticise it without understanding its purpose. It is easy to say that you should run everything back at the opposition, but that can often be a dangerous ploy. You have to remember that if you first kick the ball from your own 22, and then eventually win a line-out on the halfway line, that is a considerable gain for your team. You have won that little kicking battle. And that keeps the forwards happy. We don't like traipsing backwards as a rule!

We wanted to win that aerial battle amongst the backs. That is always something that is stressed by Rob Howley. We didn't want to kick the ball out if we could help it. We wanted to move their forwards around and work them hard. If you look at the match statistics, we kicked the ball to touch only once in the game; France did so ten times.

France had taken an early lead through a Dimitri Yachvili penalty, but then on twenty minutes came the try that was to decide the Grand Slam. Dan Lydiate had won a line-out and from there Rhys Priestland had chipped ahead. The French winger Alexis Palisson had collected and attacked. I'd tackled him low and he had off-loaded to Thierry Dusautoir, who crabbed across field. In came Dan with one of his low chop tackles on Dusautoir, and before the French flanker could do anything about it, Alun Wyn Jones had made a brilliant turnover. Referee Craig Joubert was shouting 'Turnover good!', and all of the front row – Gethin Jenkins, Matthew Rees and Adam Jones – had piled into the ruck to secure the ball.

Dan acted as scrum-half and passed the ball right to Rhys

Priestland who, with a long pass, found Alex Cuthbert out on the wing. Alex stepped inside Dusautoir who was covering across, and then between Julien Bonnaire and Yoann Maestri. Full back Clement Poitrenaud was the last line of defence, but Alex stepped inside him too with ease and we had scored our first try – our only try as it happened. Leigh Halfpenny converted and we were 7–3 up. We were never behind again in the game.

It was soon afterwards that my personal bad luck against France struck again. No one is really certain when I injured my right shoulder, but it was absolute agony. Yet everything was happening so fast that I just played on regardless. But then there was a break in play and I put my hand on my shoulder and thought, 'This is really hurting here!'

Soon there was an overthrown line-out and I went to catch it, but I simply couldn't raise my arm to do so. Bonnaire beat me to the ball. I didn't like that at all, but I just couldn't do anything about it. Then just afterwards there was a ruck where I wanted to grab hold of Dusautoir, but I just couldn't get hold of him because of my shoulder, and he ended up turning the ball over. I was so angry. Not least because I knew then that I was going to have to go off in the biggest game of my life.

Just before half-time Leigh was lining up another penalty, having made it 10–3 with one on thirty-two minutes, and I was standing behind him thinking: 'I'm going to have to go off here again.' Talk about distraught. This was my third separate injury in the Championship. I joked afterwards that 'I have to toughen up', but I was in no mood for joking at that moment.

Leigh hit the post and we went off for half-time. I saw the physios. I simply couldn't lift my arm. My game was over. There was no other option. Ryan Jones took my place and I was left to watch from the bench again.

Debutant Jean-Marcellin Buttin had replaced Poitrenaud towards the end of the first half, and he immediately made a dangerous break in the second half, chipping ahead and gaining a penalty, which Beauxis kicked to make it 10–6. But soon Dan was making yet another magnificent tackle, this time on Wesley Fofana, who was then penalised on halfway for holding on. Leigh kicked a superb penalty from just inside our half to stretch the lead to 13–6.

France were pressing hard and when Beauxis took a penalty quickly and kicked crossfield to Buttin, only Rhys Priestland and Dan were covering. Rhys slowed him up and Dan delivered the tackle. What a game he was having. Three minutes later he made an even better tackle on Buttin, smashing him so hard that the crack could be heard around the stadium!

France then had another opportunity when Imanol Harinordoquy was worked free on the right. He had a man outside him, but it was only the replacement second row Julien Pierre, so he turned back inside and was tackled by Jamie Roberts. Danger averted again.

But with eight minutes to go we were penalised at a scrum in our own 22 and Yachvili kicked it to bring it back to 13–9.

Dan was in the action again, collecting a Yachvili box kick that had gone loose, feeding Leigh, who made a superb break down the middle. The ball was moved quickly right where

Rhys Priestland grubbered ahead. Replacement Francois Trinh-Duc collected and was bundled into touch. Trinh-Duc threw the ball away and was penalised. They were rattled.

Leigh kicked the penalty and it was 16–9, with less than five minutes to go. And that was how it remained. We ran the clock down, and with the eighty-minute mark up, we were awarded a penalty. Ryan Jones, with a huge smile on his face, pointed at the time on the big screen and gave the ball to Rhys Priestland. He booted the ball into the stands and we had won the Grand Slam. It was obviously my first, but it was Wales's third in eight years. What a triumph.

That Dan was man of the match was a formality. He had put in one of the great performances, and I was so happy for him. His face looked a bit of a mess afterwards. He had some stitches, and while he hadn't broken his nose, it didn't look good at all. I just told him he looked more like me now!

As I mentioned earlier, there is always good banter between the two of us, and I am always making up nicknames for him. Quite a few like to call him 'Chopper', but I prefer 'Silent Ninja', which also refers to his remarkable tackling. He goes about his work silently and devastatingly; opponents just seem to hit the ground and you don't know why!

Dan was eventually made the official man of the Champ-ionship, but I, like most others, had already decided that well before the final whistle that day.

It had been a tough old game. France had already drawn with Ireland and lost to England, so their chance of winning the Championship had gone. But that didn't make them any less of a challenge; if anything it made them more dangerous. Their defence had caused us real problems. Their line speed had been amazing. We were playing off Mike Phillips at scrum-half, and the ball had barely left his hands before they were on us. It was very difficult to play against.

But our scramble defence had been brilliant too. There are always two ways of reacting to pressure: you can either go into your shell or come out fighting. Everybody came out fighting that day. Dan obviously stood out, but nobody played badly for us. Ian Evans had another mountainous game, and on most other days he would have been man of the match. He'd had an incredible tournament. And Alex had exploded onto the scene in his first year in top-flight rugby. With Leigh and George North he had formed a formidable back three that was only going to get better.

People were concerned about whether we'd be able to back up what we did at the World Cup. Well, we did just that. And it was such a pleasure to be involved. Everyone got on so well and it was a very happy working environment. A happy squad is a successful squad, and I think we proved that. It was easily the most enjoyable campaign I've been involved in so far. And we definitely got our just reward for all the hard work we'd put in over the previous six months.

Having said all that, it took some time for it to sink in that we were Grand Slam champions. I'd dreamt about it and seen those previous Grand Slams won on TV, but suddenly there I was out on the Millennium Stadium pitch as captain of the Wales 2012 Grand Slam champions. It felt surreal. I found myself thinking: 'Will people perceive us in the same way I perceived my heroes when I was watching them in 2005 and 2008?'

It was a brilliant feeling, but it was also rather strange, and my own situation was made stranger by the fact that I had not completed the full match. There were other players in the squad who had played almost every minute of every game. What they had put themselves through was incredible. The backs had run their legs off and the forwards were battered and bruised.

They had been training throughout the whole campaign as well, whereas I had been nursed through because I had had so many injuries. Because they had put themselves through more than me, I felt they deserved it more than me. So I felt a little awkward about going up to receive the Six Nations Championship trophy.

I mentioned this to Warren and I asked him if he might like to come up with me so that we could lift it together. He immediately said no. 'It's a players' thing,' he said. 'But if you do feel that awkward, why don't you ask Gethin and Ryan about it?'

Gethin and Ryan had, of course, also been captains during the tournament. I asked them. 'No, it's your moment, you do it,' they both replied. Fair play to them. It was a superb gesture on both their parts. Maybe they might have thought about what I went through at the World Cup. It certainly made me feel better. And they both still came up to the podium last and stood either side of me as I received the trophy from WRU chairman David Pickering.

Mind you, lifting the trophy was a bit of a problem. I could only do it with my left arm; my right arm was still no use to anybody.

After the game I had a decision to make: go for a scan immediately or wait until the Sunday morning? That was the question Professor John Williams was asking me. There were scenes of such joy that it was a tricky decision. Those are the moments a sportsperson cherishes as you enjoy each other's company in celebration of such a huge achievement. The music was blaring in the changing rooms as the trophy was brought in and a series of photos was done.

Then it was off to the family room to see my parents and Rachel, where there were more wonderfully happy photos taken. It was an amazing feeling. Next was a special photo out on the pitch with the squad dressed smartly in their dinner suits; definitely one to remember.

But I'd decided that I wanted a scan that night. I wanted to know how bad it was. It felt bad, but I needed to know exactly what I'd done. I couldn't have enjoyed my night otherwise.

The scan only took twenty minutes, and with a twenty-minute journey to and from the Spire Hospital in Pentwyn, Cardiff, I was back at the Hilton Hotel in time for the after-match function.

I went with Prof and with Ryan Jones, who was also going for a scan. I'm not sure what was wrong with him. I think he admitted afterwards that it was nothing!

Anyone who has had an MRI scan will know that they are

not particularly pleasant, especially if you happen to be a little bit claustrophobic. You lie there in a very small tunnel with your only company the voice of the radiographer coming through your headphones. 'Next scan now. This will last five minutes,' he will say.

What he does not usually say is: 'Warby, you faggot, there is nothing wrong with you!' But that was what I was suddenly hearing through my headphones as my scan came to an end. 'It's only a bruise. I've got some man-up pills for you in the car if you want,' the voice continued.

It was Ryan. And even in that horrible tunnel I had to laugh.

I'll admit that I didn't laugh when I saw Prof and Ryan afterwards. 'It's only showing up as a bruise,' said Prof.

What, there was no structural damage? I couldn't move my arm and there was nothing seriously wrong with it? It just didn't seem right. I wasn't questioning Prof's vast medical knowledge – he was only relaying the message that the scans had revealed – but I was gobsmacked.

All the while Ryan was giggling away. 'You're meant to be captain of Wales, Warby,' he laughed. 'And you have to go off at half-time again when there is nothing wrong with you! I can't wait to tell the boys.'

I took it all in good humour. But I knew it was more than a bruise. And subsequently it was found that I had some serious nerve damage to my shoulder. I did not play again during the domestic season, only returning eleven weeks later for the first Test in Australia in early June.

*

I was in good spirits when we got back to the Hilton Hotel for that after-match function. I was also in a slightly mischievous mood. It was Matthew Rees's fiftieth cap and I thought it might be nice if he sang a song for us. It is, of course, the tradition that a new cap sings a song. That usually happens on the team bus, but when Aaron Shingler and Lou Reed had made their debuts against Scotland earlier in the tournament, Mike Phillips had begun winding them up, saying that they would have to sing at the after-match function when all the sponsors and officials were present.

And that's what happened. Aaron was going to sing 'In Da Club' by 50 Cent, but when he saw the audience he quite rightly realised that the lyrics would not be appropriate. So instead he sang Robbie Williams's 'Angels' and all the boys joined in. It was sensational.

As for Lou Reed, well, with a name like that, what do you expect? He can sing. He sang Lionel Richie's 'Hello' and received a standing ovation.

Both of them were miles better than I had been on my debut in America in 2009. As I've already mentioned, I don't like singing. So I spent the whole week before the match learning the lyrics of 'Wonderwall' by Oasis. I know that sounds a boring choice, but the truth was that the lyrics were the easiest to learn. And I found myself worrying about singing it when the match was going on!

All the boys were keen for Matthew to sing. They were chanting his nickname: 'Smiler! Smiler!' I even tried to send him on a bit of a guilt trip by standing up and saying (no problems with public speaking now!), 'When I was first asked to be captain, I didn't really want to be captain. But Matthew sat me down and gave me some great advice. He told me that I had to try to keep the boys happy off the field and that I should lead by example. So that's why I think he should sing a song for his fiftieth cap!'

It didn't work. He still wouldn't sing. But we had a great night. And yes, I did have a few cranberry vodkas. If you can't celebrate a Grand Slam, when can you celebrate?

We had a good sing-song in the bar in the Hilton Hotel after all the formal stuff had ended. We even got France's replacement hooker Dimitri Szarzewski to come into the middle of our circle and sing for us. We had no idea what he was singing, but we thought he looked like a better-looking version of Richard Hibbard! 'Sexy Hibbs', the boys were calling him.

Wayne Barnes, who was a touch judge that day, was also persuaded to come over and sing for us. We kept grabbing him as he was going to the toilet, so he relented and we were all chanting 'Barnesy! Barnesy!' as he sang.

We then headed off into town. It was absolute chaos, but I had promised that I would meet my brother as well as a couple of other mates, David Rowlands and James Perkins. So I walked to the Revolution bar with Rachel. As we arrived there, George North was coming out with his girlfriend, the cyclist Becky James. 'Don't go in there,' he said. 'It's carnage! I'm knocking it on the head.'

But we did go in. And we did find a relatively quiet spot around the back of the bar. We had a good time and had some good banter with a group of French fans. And then it was time to get back to the hotel on the bus laid on for us at 3am. Rachel and I went back with Dan and his girlfriend Nia, and one of the team analysts Andrew Hughes and his wife Natalie.

It had been a great day and a great night. Most of us had gone our separate ways after the Hilton, but there had been no trouble whatsoever. That was pleasing. The players had not been as crazy as they might have been before. Everyone understood that having just won a Grand Slam, they wouldn't want to let themselves down by doing something silly.

There were only two things left to do. First was a huge fry-up at the team hotel on the Sunday morning. That is always our reward at the end of a campaign, and we felt that it was fully deserved.

And second was a visit to the Senedd, the National Assembly building in Cardiff Bay, on the Monday evening after the game. It had been announced after the match on the Saturday that we had been invited there by the Welsh Government and Cardiff City Council. But when we boarded the team bus at the Vale Hotel, we had no idea how big a deal this was going to be.

The first priority was to talk to Ryan Bevington. He had just proposed to his girlfriend, Lucy. There were congratulations flying around, but from me all he got was: 'Bevs, you're killing me!'

Why? Because Lucy is very close to Rachel, as well as Dan's girlfriend Nia, and Scott Williams's girlfriend Tanya. Ryan's proposal had certainly cranked up the pressure on the rest of us! And just after I'd seen Bevs, Dan came onto the bus and said exactly the same thing: 'You're killing me!' Moments later Scott appeared. Yes, guess what he said too! We were only joking, honestly.

Of course we were, because in July I followed Bev's lead, proposing to Rachel while we were down in west Wales. I got down on one knee – nice and traditional – and there were tears. When she stopped crying she eventually said yes. And I've named our house after the spot where I proposed, which has gone down well, although the proposal nearly wasn't a surprise. I went to buy a ring and obviously didn't want anyone to see me. So as I was having a quick look in the shop window before going in, a random guy walked past and said, 'Make sure you spend your money, Mr Warburton!' I hurried in!

Anyway, back to the Senedd. How many people would turn up? It is always a worry at these sorts of functions. If nobody turns up, it can look very embarrassing. But we shouldn't have worried when we know how wonderful our fans are.

There were thousands of people waiting for us. It was estimated that there were 8,000 of them. The scenes were incredible.

I hadn't realised that the presentation of the Six Nations trophy by First Minister Carwyn Jones was going to be shown live on TV, so I quickly phoned Rachel and asked her to tape it. We walked out and it was like being in a rock band, with the crowd stretched out in front of us across the bay.

Just before he handed over the trophy to me, the First Minister said: 'What we have here is a great team, a great captain and a great coach. It gives me great pleasure to present the trophy to the Triple Crown and Grand Slam champions, Cymru – Wales.'

And then the fireworks and ticker tape were let off with a huge bang. Warren Gatland, standing to my right, nearly jumped out of his skin! The boys found it hilarious. Even with the noise of the crowd I could hear their laughter behind me. Warren had been warned about it, but he obviously didn't think it would be that loud.

There were lots of photos and interviews then, and finally it was time to board the bus. I was the last to do so, and as I walked towards it, there were hundreds of people, mainly children, screaming at me, holding out their programmes and jerseys and other stuff to be signed. Everyone was on the bus waiting for me. I had two security guards with me, and they were telling me not to stop.

But I really wanted to stop. I felt bad about letting all those children down. I don't like doing that. So I apologise now to anyone who was there that night and did not get my autograph. Please come to a Cardiff Blues game and I'll do it for you. I always do that after games for the Blues.

So I got on the bus, and that was it. Back to the hotel, and, quite literally, the end of our Grand Slam journey.

Who would have thought that when I first received that call from Warren Gatland asking me to be captain against the Barbarians, under a year later I would be a Grand Slam-winning captain?

It had been some journey.

It had been some year.

Acknowledgements

I would like to thank the following for their help in producing this book: Simon & Schuster for their enthusiasm throughout the project, and Steve James for helping me to put it together.

I would also like to thank the following for all their help and support during the year that began with my captaining of Wales against the Barbarians in June 2011 and ended with the winning of the Grand Slam in March 2012: my agent Derwyn Jones for his constant support and great advice over the past four years, Andy McCann for supporting me through the last few years and for helping me play my best rugby, Warren Gatland and all the management team at the Welsh Rugby Union for their hard work and professionalism, and all my teammates for their excellence and camaraderie.

Last, but of course not least, a huge thank you to all my family – especially Mum, Dad, my brother Ben and sister Holly, and my girlfriend Rachel who has had to put up with me for the last twelve months! Thanks for coming to all of my games; none of this would have been possible without all of your support.